The Attention Economy and How Media Works

Karen Nelson-Field

The Attention Economy and How Media Works

Simple Truths for Marketers

Karen Nelson-Field
Amplified Intelligence Pty Ltd
Adelaide, SA, Australia

ISBN 978-981-15-1539-2 ISBN 978-981-15-1540-8 (eBook)
https://doi.org/10.1007/978-981-15-1540-8

This Palgrave Macmillan imprint is published by the registered company Springer Nature Singapore Pte Ltd.
The registered company address is: 152 Beach Road, #21-01/04 Gateway East, Singapore 189721, Singapore

Foreword

Today's world has gotten a lot noisier. Marketing messages are not only competing with other advertising, but also the latest adorable pet video, celebrity tweet, and 'break the internet' moment of the day. With competition at an all-time high for people's attention, marketing professionals are faced with a challenge that's impossible to ignore: how do we evolve our decision making in today's data-rich world to cut through all of the noise?

To get to the root of understanding human behaviour and what drives our impulses, my team at Mars shares Karen's belief that we need a scientific approach to critically navigate the data-rich, attention-poor media environment. Our unique approach to behavioural advertising research is equally championed by the academic world and by the practitioner's world, and we salute Karen's long standing, robust contributions to unpacking this complex subject.

In this book, Karen tackles the rapidly changing media environment, creating a healthy debate on what it takes for businesses to win in the new attention economy. In a world where misinformation often spreads fastest and loudest, Karen's voice is an important one. It's the voice of discovering our true north, through objective theory that's fundamentally grounded in scientific, behavioural measurement and sound methodology. Karen brings a unique perspective to examining these challenges from both a data-driven and human-centric perspective. Her work provides evidence-based answers to the media questions businesses are faced with daily, distilling them down into simple truths regarding the impact of rapidly evolving technology and the new challenges this creates for advertisers as we look to the future.

Karen's writing is a great opportunity to tune out the noise and tune in to valuable insights on marketing. It deserves all your attention.

Laurent Larguinat
Senior Director, Mars Consumer
and Market Insights
Brussels, Belgium

Acknowledgements

For My Team

This book is certainly not a lone effort, rather it was built on the shoulders of a very special group. Our worlds and expertise vary so drastically but our seemingly eclectic group is pure gold and produces brilliant work. When I think about how far we have come in such a short time, and the global recognition we are afforded, I am so proud. When I think about how much fun we have in the office, and many 'roll-on-floor' laughing moments we've had along the way, I am equally proud. Fun is good. So thank you to Dylan Lundy, Melissa Banelis, Carole Lydon, Brandon Matthews, Miguel Martin, Daniel Lyas, Erica Riebe, Kellen Ewens and Pippi Nottage. And thank you to our extended team of contractors who support us.

For My Family

Boys, oops!…I did it again. I promised I wouldn't lock myself in an office to write a book and not feed you for extended periods again, but it happened. Thank you Connor and Alec for being big enough now to cook your own two-minute noodles (and for being awesome kids regardless of not actually understanding what your Mum does for a living).

Pete, it is so nice to put you in a publication dedication knowing I won't regret it. Your husband skills are without a doubt of the highest calibre and it is thanks to these skills that I can be the complicated person that I am and write these complicated books.

Thank you family, much love to you.

Contents

Notes on Contributors

Stuart Bailey is an industry leader with over 18 years' experience across the UK and Australia. Over his career, he has worked in business management, digital, trading and at an executive level at leading global media agencies giving him a full spectrum perspective of the industry. He is a specialist at transforming digital offerings and cultures and accelerating client's digital capabilities. Currently, Stuart is Chief Digital Officer at PHD Australia where he is evolving the digital product, championing education, driving key client's digital acceleration as well as delivering thought leadership on key industry topics.

Dr. Augustine Fou is an independent cybersecurity and ad fraud researcher who helps clients identify and remove fraud impacting their marketing campaigns. He is an industry-recognised thought leader in digital strategy and integrated marketing. Dr. Fou was the former Chief Digital Officer of Omnicom's Healthcare Consultancy Group, a US$100 million agency group serving pharma, medical device and healthcare clients. He has also served as SVP, digital strategy lead, at McCann Worldgroup/MRM Worldwide. Dr. Fou taught digital strategy at NYU's School of Continuing and Professional Studies and Rutgers University's Center for Management Development. He started his career in New York City with McKinsey & Company.

Professor Wolfgang Henseler is the founder and the managing creative director of SENSORY-MINDS, a design studio for new media and innovative technologies based in Offenbach, Germany. He is also a Professor for Digital Media and an expert in digital transformation, user centricity and user experience and the Dean for Intermedia Design (the design of smart objects and the Internet of Things) at the University of Pforzheim/Germany, Faculty for Design.

Bob Hoffman is the author of four Amazon #1 selling books about advertising. He is also one of the most sought-after international speakers on advertising and marketing. He has brought us The Ad Contrarian blog since 2007. Bob has been the CEO of two independent agencies and the US operation of an international agency. In 2012 he was selected 'Ad Person of the Year' by the San Francisco Advertising Club. His commentary has appeared in the *BBC World Service*, *The Wall Street Journal*, *MSNBC*, *The Financial Times*, *The Australian*, *New Zealand Public Broadcasting*, *Fox News*, *Sky News*, *Forbes*, *Canadian Public Broadcasting*, and many other news outlets throughout the world.

Professor Jared Horvath (Ph.D., M.Ed.) is a neuroscientist, educator and author of the best-selling book *Stop Talking, Start Influencing: 12 Insights from Brain Science to Make Your Message Stick*. He has conducted research and lectured at Harvard University, Harvard Medical School, the University of Melbourne and over 150 schools internationally. He currently serves as the Director of LME Global: a team dedicated to bringing the latest brain and behavioural research to teachers, students and parents alike.

Carole Lydon started in local government collecting numbers and writing about them to win funding or keep the authorities happy. She then moved to the glamourous world of law firm marketing and came out the other side a wily shadow of her former self. From there, her debilitating sense of curiosity drove her freelance work as a writer/editor. Carole edited Karen Nelson-Field's first book, *Viral Marketing: The Science of Sharing* in 2012. She joined Amplified Intelligence in 2018 as chief word wrangler.

Dr. Karen Nelson-Field (Ph.D.) is the Founder and Executive Director of Amplified Intelligence and Professor of Media Innovation at The University of Adelaide. Karen is a globally acclaimed researcher in media science, is a regular speaker on the major circuits and has secured research funding from some of the world's largest advertisers. Her first book, *Viral Marketing: The Science of Sharing*, set the record straight on hunting for 'viral success'. Her work has been noted in *The New York Times*, *Bloomberg Business*, *CNBC*, *Forbes*, *Wall Street Journal*, *Huffington Post*, *Contagious* and *The Drum*, and she is a regular media writer for the *Australian Financial Review*. Karen's commercial work combines tech and innovative methodological design to look closely at attention metrics in a disrupting digital economy.

Wiemer Snijders is the managing editor *Eat Your Greens: Fact-Based Thinking to Improve Your Brand's Health* and a regular keynote speaker on the topic of marketing science. He is a partner at The Commercial Works, where he offers research and advisory services centred on using the fundamentals of buyer behaviour to make marketing simpler—and his clients more successful. He works for clients in various countries from a broad range of industries in business-to-consumer and business-to-business markets.

Schalk van der Sandt has experience in digital media that stretches back to 2001, and his roles span across both brand and media agency. Most recently he has led the digital product for PHD Australia in Melbourne, where he has worked with some of Australia's biggest brands on their transitions into the digital and programmatic era.

List of Figures

List of Tables

1

State of Play

Three-quarters of our business comes from stuff that Don Draper wouldn't have recognized 30 years ago. We probably wouldn't have recognized it ourselves 15 years ago.

Sir Martin Sorrell, Founder, WPP

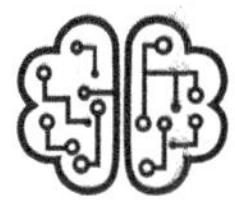

There's no need for a long drawn out description of the history of commercial media. All you need to know is that until the noughties, media evolved steadily and in line with technology, from town crier to the Gutenberg Press to radio to television to direct response to cable to the internet. And the past 15 years have offered some moments in time that represent critical change to the fate of our industry. A period that has brought chaos to the CMO like no other time in marketing. A period where brands have been made and broken. Not even Don Draper could have foreseen this level of change, nor could he have recommended how marketers should respond. He was a simple ad guy in a simple time.

K. Nelson-Field, *The Attention Economy and How Media Works*,
https://doi.org/10.1007/978-981-15-1540-8_1

1.1 Critical Media Moments in Time

1.1.1 Blitzscaling and the Accidental Media Companies

It took television 30 years to go from black and white to colour, yet in a little over five years Mark Zuckerberg took a website called FaceMash to one of the biggest media brands in history. Within six years of launch it was amassing 400 million people a month. Welcome to 'blitzscaling'. A concept coined by Reid Hoffman (co-founder LinkedIn) around the idea of how companies attain explosive growth, lightning fast. It is about doing and building things others won't, and thinking unconventionally about rules, risk and pivoting. It is a 10% growth per day thing, not 10% growth per year (which is better than most marketers could dream).

Hoffman cautions that the approach is not for the light-hearted. Not everyone has the stomach for this type of thinking. In a high-stakes winner-takes-all game, losing foretells of biblical proportions. Netscape were perhaps one of the earliest examples of blitzscaling, rising to an eye watering US$2 billion market cap in 16 months, but they are also an example of falling hard. Within ten years of its establishment the browser service went from 90% market share to less than 1% in 2006. Regardless, Netscape made its mark on the world.

In the noughties several websites out of the pioneering Silicon Valley went from zero customers to a gazillion in record time. And the value of these customers' eyeballs was quickly realised. Creating a commercial online media platform became the new business model, even when the original plan may not have been. Zuckerberg famously held back on commercialising advertising until four years after the business began. His initial focus, he claims, was more on connecting everyone in the world and less about the advertising opportunity. He talked about taking on advertising to pay the bills. Sheryl Sandberg, in 2008, saw advertising for the opportunity it was. YouTube, in its youth, was an innocent place dedicated to a small group of creators motivated by their art. In 2006, less than 12 months later, it was sold to Google and advertising monetisation began two years after its launch. It's hard to believe, but in the early days Google was opposed to advertising-supported search engines due to the bias it may bestow. Amazon started as an online trader, with a slower evolution to becoming an ad seller. Now it is fast on its way to becoming one of the biggest media companies in the world. None of these company's missions have changed, but the definition of what constitutes a customer sure has. They are in the business of attracting the attention of customers and re-selling it.

In less than five years the marketplace was filled with gargantuan advertising opportunities on social, search, video and microblogging. This was the first time in history marketers could easily access global reach in one place; providing an answer to the fragmentation problem of the eighties and nineties. Consequently, over a few short years the shift in advertising spending away from traditional platforms to new media was about as epic as blitzscaling itself.

Not surprisingly, the scale of this disruption has had its consequences on the broader industry. Fundamental shifts are never easy. In 2018, complaints were made to the Australian Competition and Consumer Commission (ACCC) arguing that the digital duopoly (Facebook and YouTube) were 'rule bending' and should be more closely scrutinised by regulators (as the traditional platforms have been). This included complaints regarding the facilitation of content piracy, lack of transparency for measurement, and data aggregation. These are weighty complaints. The piracy claims were based on platforms not providing any financial contribution towards TV content being viewed on social sites. Data aggregation becomes a problem when critical mass restricts new entrants into the marketplace. But perhaps the most talked about issue in advertising circles is measurement transparency. A lack of transparency over the algorithms, makes it difficult for competition regulators around the world to assess anti-competitive conduct. Since then a USA congressional inquisition expressed concern for privacy and monopolisation from Facebook, while EU countries have launched legal challenges on Google and Facebook for privacy and anti-trust practices.

The point here is to demonstrate that rule bending is a classic blitzscale technique without which these companies wouldn't exist. And this rule bending has literally changed everything about media and advertising (and life as we know it more generally). We have information organisers, video sharers, social and professional networkers, auctioneers and news gatherers all now sitting safely in the media owner category (although for regulatory purposes, some refute that they are). This is a category that has been dominated by a select few for many decades.

QUICK EXPLAINER

The ACCC Digital Platforms Inquiry

The Australian Competition and Consumer Commission (ACCC) is an independent Commonwealth statutory authority whose role is to enforce the Competition and Consumer Act 2010. As well as a range of additional legislation, promoting competition, fair trading and regulating national infrastructure for the benefit of all Australians.

On 4 December 2017, the then Treasurer, the Hon Scott Morrison MP, directed the ACCC to conduct an inquiry into digital platforms. The inquiry looked at the effect that digital search engines, social media platforms and other digital content aggregation platforms have on competition in media and advertising services markets. In particular, the inquiry looked at the impact of digital platforms on the supply of news and journalistic content, and the implications of this for media content creators, advertisers and consumers.

The final report was published on 26 July 2019.

The ACCC suggested that the dominance of the leading digital platforms and their impact across Australia's economy, media and society must be addressed with significant, holistic reform.

The wide-reaching report contains 23 recommendations, spanning competition law (the ability for other media businesses to compete), consumer protection and privacy law (control over usage and collection of personal data) and media regulation (disinformation and a rising mistrust of news).

As at October 2019, the Australian government was considering all recommendations.

See the final report here: https://www.accc.gov.au/publications/digital-platforms-inquiry-final-report.

1.1.2 Free Reach and Going Viral

The next critical media moment in time involves kittens and babies. You've heard it before. Put a cute baby in a video and it will go viral. Kittens on roller skates will spread video content wildly from a small base on the internet through social and email. Unfortunately, the term *viral* is one of the most grossly misused marketing words today. The term was catapulted by the meteoric rise of YouTube after Google bought the company in 2006. Unlike watching traditional video on TV, users were encouraged to engage in the content by way of commenting, rating, favouriting and, of course, sharing to other users. Now, *going viral* carries its own identity beyond YouTube and is used for just about any content sharing on any media site—word-of-mouth on steroids.

As a medical term, viral has been used for at least 300 years, most often during an epidemic to describe the spread of a virus from a single host to many people. Like many marketing terms borrowed from other sectors, viral is loosely understood and even more loosely measured. The concept of going viral is a function of time and the rate of sharing—the rate of sharing means the ratio between number of views to number of shares. For a video to be truly viral, this ratio needs to present as views < shares. In layman's terms, one person views the video which results in many more people sharing. As such, the concept of viral has borne the impression that online video advertising will bring you free reach—that if we build it (and upload it) they will come in droves without additional cost (or the need to invest in reach at all).

As word-of-mouth on steroids, the viral concept is flawed by the natural shape of content distribution (a reverse J-shape curve). The reality is, and our own extensive work has proven, that the likelihood of a video spreading to millions from a small seed is highly unlikely, and upfront paid seeding plays a bigger role than most people think. Nevertheless, *going viral* has catapulted us into the world of earned media where marketers are seduced by the free eyeballs lottery. This is the critical media moment in time that turned marketers into gamblers, and like real gamblers they ignore the fact that the odds are stacked against them.

REMEMBER THIS SIMPLE TRUTH

The concept of viral marketing is utterly flawed by the nature of the shape of the sharing distribution.

1.1.3 Instant Measurement Appeared in an Instant

The first rule of social software design is that more engagement is better, and that the way you get engagement is by adding stuff like Like buttons and notifications.

James Somers, Contributing Editor, The Atlantic Boston

In the mid-noughties, Justin Rosenstein delivered a masterstroke for Facebook, co-inventing the Like button and single-handedly changing the nature of how we consider advertising success. While other metrics (such as, views, shares, comments, ratings) had been introduced on YouTube a few years earlier, the Facebook Like button was the first time customer approval was directly linked to a brand (as opposed to content) at such scale. In the early days Like was literally taken as being a fan of the brand. In my own research at the time we debunked this myth showing that in an average week less than 1% of the brand fans bothered to return to the page they had Liked. Since then, Liking has become more widespread along with its other engagement cousins—followers, visitors, viewing minutes, reactions, retweets, favourites, watch list, mentions, dislikes, clicks, shares, views, comments and the list goes on (and on). These are all favourite online volume metrics used to measure the success of online campaigns.

But there are no unicorns and glitter in Fight Club. And two highly significant (negative) flow-on effects resulted from the adoption of instant measurement.

First, the rise of short-termism. With easy access, marketers have become addicted to instant measurement (no real surprises there). What this means is that they have switched focus from investing in and measuring, longer term brand impacts. The new focus has prompted fleeting campaigns that see immediate spikes in sales and have easily accessible ROI metrics. Traditional advertising research takes time for a number of reasons, including (but not limited to) the need for complicated experimental and sample controls. Lack of measurement controls means that online engagement metrics are often skewed by market share giving an uneven representation of buyer distribution. For example, big brands have more buyers, so engagement volume from a bigger brand might look acceptable on the surface, but in reality the brand could be underperforming for its size. Actual volume doesn't tell the whole story. Heavy buyers typically respond to short-term campaigns and are more likely to engage in liking/sharing/commenting in brand communities. Engagement from these customers is expected and tells us nothing about brand growth potential.

Secondly, our obsession with and willingness to pay for instant measurement has impelled the ugly world of ad fraud at eye-watering scale (more on this in Chapter 8). There are two common types of ad fraud—impression fraud and click fraud. Instant measurement has given the green light to both. Thanks to advertisers' obsession with short-term metrics, a whole underground (illegal) market has emerged to falsify their volume.

Instant measurement provides no good outcome for the advertiser. Either they pay for fake engagement or, perhaps worse, the metrics they rely on for campaign effectiveness have no rigorous base. History has taught us that sometimes the flow-on effects from a discovery are far more powerful and pervasive than the original event. When nuclear fission was discovered in 1938 by Otto Hahn and Fritz Strassmann, they couldn't have imagined where it would end up. It took until 1952 for the Americans to test their first nuclear weapon. Now in 2019, nine countries have over 15,000 nuclear weapons. While not nuclear, the scale of instant measurement is massive and its flow-on effects bestow a far greater critical moment in media than its initial development.

1.1.4 The Machines Arrived

In the midst of the blitzscaling boom media buying automation arrived, and the purchase of Double Click by Google ignited an era of programmatic trading. Suddenly the manual processing of buying media was taken away from humans and given to *much smarter* computers to automate which ads to buy and how much to pay for them (more in Chapter 4). Programmatic started as a way of using up remnant digital inventory but it has evolved to become the very soul of real-time online targeting. Real-time online targeting means advertisers can now access target customers anywhere in the world in the very instant they display online buying cues. It is opportunistic and it capitalises on intent (or signals thereof). It *reportedly* offers marketers the opportunity to accurately apply the principles of recency (see Chapter 8).

In theory this is gold. In reality, it encouraged brands away from marketing to many people, to mining for fewer people in a hyper-relevant way. This added more fuel to the damaging obsession with instant everything and short-term thinking. While Google pioneered the targeted advertising business model in the late 1990s, Sheryl Sandberg didn't introduce it to Facebook until 2008.

As if by sliding doors, Jon Mandel broke the ad agency model in the mid-2000s. Jon Mandel was a heavy hitting agency CEO who lifted the lid on agency rebates, kickbacks and all things transparency and trust. What followed from his whistleblowing speech was nothing short of a category 5 hurricane. Firstly, approximately US$50 billion of accounts were put up for review, then a second wave of disintermediation is said to have occurred when advertisers started going direct to online publishers. The online publishers readily embraced this by ramping up operations to focus on direct relationships with advertisers (and their data). It was perfect timing for the growth and commercialisation of online targeting. As a consequence, Google and Facebook are now said to bank some of the richest first and second party data in the world.

And bang, this is a super critical moment in media history. The assignment of power to a few main players in digital. Those who own the data, own the world.

QUICK EXPLAINER

Trying harder as the underdog

'We Try Harder' was a famous Avis car rental print campaign in the 1960s and 1970s that changed their fortune. The campaign debuted in 1962 when Avis was dominated by the number one in the market, Hertz, and at a time when Avis was not turning profit. Doyle Dane Bernbach (now known as DDB) was employed to help. Knowing Hertz was light years away in terms of market share, the objective of the campaign was to embrace their second-place position to turn the business around. Bill Bernbach, the co-founder of DDB, asked management why anyone ever rents a car from them. Their response, 'because we try harder', then became a promise to their consumers about the quality of service. The famous tag line was born and it elevated the brand's status to the point that in one year the company went from losing US$3.2 million to turning a profit of US$1.2 million for the first time in 13 years.

In 2012, after nearly 50 years, Avis dropped the distinctive tag line for something that promises consumers nothing and is much less memorable, 'It's Your Space'. That CMO has come and gone.

1.1.5 Hyper-Personalisation (aka Web of One)

When Facebook or Google point their supercomputers toward our minds, it's checkmate.

Tristan Harris, Founder, Center for Humane Technology

There is a painfully awkward conversation between Dr. Evil and Frau in *Austin Powers: The Spy Who Shagged Me* (1999, New Line Cinema) after their one-time sexual encounter, where Dr. Evil states the obvious to Frau, 'It got weird didn't it?'. Well perhaps the next critical media moment in time can be explained in the same way—it got weird.

From a place of good intention, real-time targeting went from technology that could find groups of target customers for the purpose of marketing efficiency, to hyper-personalisation algorithms that monitor you on and offline 24/7. Your phone, IoT devices, and smart TV know every single thing about you and your friends, for the sole purpose of predicting your next move. All in the name of marketing efficiency.

Surveillance capitalism becomes the tool for hyper-personalisation.

Professor Shoshana Zuboff, a subject matter expert on surveillance capitalism, talks about the level of monitoring online being akin to criminal. She says, 'Most Americans realize that there are two groups of people who are monitored regularly as they move about the country. The first group is monitored involuntarily by a court order requiring that a tracking device be attached to their ankle. The second group includes everyone else…Just like 20th century firms like General Motors and Ford invented mass production and managerial capitalism, Google and Facebook figured out how to commodify 'reality' itself by tracking what people (and not just their users) do online (and increasingly offline too), making predictions about what they might do in the future, devising ways to influence behaviour from shopping to voting, and selling that power to whoever is willing to pay.'

But our conversation is not about the legal, ethical, social, political rights and wrongs of surveillance capitalism. There are plenty of ex-Google/Facebook/Mozilla employees happy to talk and write about that—Ken Auletta, Roger McNamee, James Williams, Tristan Harris, Aza Raskin. This conversation is about what it might mean for brands.

Let's start with the *The Filter Bubble*. Even back in 2011, Eli Pariser, a political and internet activist, started talking about invisible algorithmic editing and information control. He is less finger pointing than some other activists. He talks more broadly about how filter bubbles are formed, often with a skewed look of life, when an algorithm chooses what you see and what you don't see.

He argues that before the internet we were controlled by editors of news who decided what we saw/read/heard and what we didn't. Then along came the internet and we all felt liberated but, he argues, we are not. There is a passing of the control torch from human editors to algorithmic editors. And filter bubbles are formed, Pariser describes, when we don't see a balance of Homelessness AND The Oscars, the war in Afghanistan AND Justin Bieber, people like you AND different people. More recent activists in this space speak of the same bubbles, acknowledging that bubbles are a pre-disposition in someone's mind and the nature of the algorithm (at times wrongly) confirms the idea.

It's easy for things to get weird when your social reference points are removed or manipulated (that's how a cult works). That's why Frau loves Dr. Evil, yet he is actually evil and wants to rule the world. But filter bubbles are good for the commoditisation of attention. The online platforms want Frau to love Dr. Evil, and they don't want to show her content that makes her think otherwise.

Hyper-personalisation is still in its (relative) infancy and its first real game-changing application is the new retail model (Amazon model). Real-time personalisation engines within an e-commerce platform move us from actively seeking out/shopping to functional buying. These algorithms narrow down our choices making decisions based on previous first choice and wants. It weeds out the 'purported' clutter. When this happens two things disappear: curation of information and the importance of needs over wants. Is this where we are headed with all hyper-personalisation marketing? How do brands navigate this new model? Does traditional marketing, and repertoire buying, fit in? Do they simply need to nail product quality, physical distribution and customer user experience?

That takes us back to a 1950s scenario. You drive a Chevrolet. The dealer is in your local town, he knows what you need and want. He can deliver it to you. But of course, in those days, if you had a falling out with the Chevrolet dealer you drove to the next town and went to their dealer. Now, there is no next town. So, are function and distribution the new norm? Where distribution means tactical negotiation with algorithm owners and this becomes the new shelf space planning?

When you look under the hood of the Amazon search engine ranking algorithm (as much as the public can) there are a number of things that challenge the current advertising charter.

Their number one end-goal is degree of sales conversion over time, which is not overly surprising, but they reward brands (with ranking) that achieve more of this. This means those who achieve greater sales velocity relative to their competition for the same search term win the higher ranking (i.e. recent [weighted] vs. lifetime sales velocity). Those who gain higher ranking also close the loop on the bubbles. It becomes self-fulfilling: big brands have more customers who buy more often. Without even trying, big brands win. So, what does this model do for the future of small brands? Will small brands die and big brands get bigger? Or perhaps big brands won't get bigger because user relevancy plays a role in the search term, so we would expect that sales on this site will come more from heavier buyers than from light buyers. Also, Amazon rewards brands (with higher ranking) who advertise within their ecosystem. Again, not so surprising. Not only does this foster big brands again (because they have more money to advertise), but it also challenges the nature of creative and branded content as we know it. They make it very clear you are creating ads for the machine first, human second.

So many questions, not many answers. And here are some more.

If humans are noted to be impacted by the skew of the editorial, will some brands naturally never earn exposure? Will competition law, consumer protection and privacy law force a day of reckoning? Will there be an AdTech crash?

And the big one, will laws of brand growth hold? More on this in Chapter 2.

The only thing we know for sure is that no-one knows the answers. We need future-facing research agendas that help us navigate all these questions.

We don't need filtered information from those who stand to make the most commercially from their answers. Plus, we do know for sure that targeting got weird.

Make sure you read Chapter 9 for a considered glimpse into the future.

1.2 What Have These Critical Moments Done to the Advertising Troops?

1.2.1 Factfulness and Confusion

Over the past 15 years everything has changed about advertising and media, or has it? Is it possible that the marketing we practised before the blitzscaling period doesn't apply?

Do we have a grasp of both sides? Unlikely. Could we be living in a bubble? Most likely.

A book I whole-heartedly recommend is called *Factfulness: Ten Reasons We're Wrong About the World and Why Things Are Better Than You Think*. The author is Hans Rosling, a Harvard Humanitarian Award winning medical doctor, Professor of International Health, and one of Time Magazine's 100 most influential people in the world. The book was his last-ditch effort to fight global ignorance and calm fears before he died in 2017. It is about perception versus reality, fact versus opinion, generally how humans live in a bubble of mega misconception about how the world really works. Remarkably, it was written before the time when curation of information was controlled by algorithmic editors.

Professor Rosling's major thesis is that as humans we overdramatise stories resulting in the very large majority of us (around 86%) interpreting the world devastatingly and systematically wrong. Like the way we (some of us) feel the 1970s was a much better time to grow up. But in reality, when we consider the facts around increased access to education, reduced deaths from cancer, greater rate of democracy etc., it wasn't. He calls the concept *Factfulness* versus *Fact-based.* Rosling suggests there are a few reasons why humans are Factful. One being our tendency to think in a binary way when a vast gap exists between extremes. Or, our lack of capacity to process large amounts of information so that only the dramatic shouty headlines get past our attention filter. Perhaps the reason most relevant to the marketing industry is the concept of *the view from up here.* A concept where people on the upper level of society honestly have no concept of how the other side live.

While Rosling was talking specifically about the rich and poor, the analogy can be applied to any divided population where those in a bubble might think they understand those outside the bubble. When really they don't.

Advertisers operate in a state of Factfulness, where opinion is rife over facts. There are studies that show bubble thinking in the context of audience consumption. Three separate large-scale studies run in 2016 (UK) and 2017 (Australia, Canada), considered how advertising professionals (AdLand) perceive the media consumption habits of *normal* people, then cross compared to the reality, based on actual data. The AdLand sample comprised advertisers, media agencies, creative agencies and media owners. The findings were strikingly similar for each country. It would seem the inhabitants of AdLand grossly overestimate the online media consumption of normal people (consumption of Facebook, YouTube, Twitter, Snapchat, Instagram), while these same people significantly underestimated time spent viewing on TV.

It's not about which platform wins a prize. The point is that when one group lives in a vastly different manner to another, a bubble appears and perceptions of the other half can be wrong. Facebook and YouTube, in particular, are exceptional and consistent purveyors of their own value (TV not so much). They run programs where staff are placed within advertising agencies for the direct purpose of teaching advertisers how to advertise on their platforms. It's not surprising perceptions of those in AdLand are out of whack.

Next, Wiemer Snijders presents bubble thinking in the context of brand growth.

1.2.2 Confusion is Driving us to the Right (Not Left) Side of the Banana

By Wiemer Snijders

Being out of touch with consumers is one thing, and of course it's not ideal if it's your job to sell to them, but marketers also seem out of touch with themselves.

Since 2008, twice a year a large group of Chief Marketing Officers (CMOs) is asked about their outlook on a broad range of topics in what is called the CMO Survey. It is sponsored by prominent companies such as Deloitte, the American Marketing Association, and the Fuqua School of Business. It is widely promoted in trade publications as a guide on what to expect in our crazy marketing world. But how much value should we place on what marketers think? Do these predictions come true? Casting our gaze back to some previous predictions can prove interesting. For example, in 2014 the survey results predicted that expected spending on social media would rise to 25% of their total budget in five years. Yet in 2019 spending on social media remained at a stable 10%.

Expectations (and predictions) often fall very short of reality. To be honest this is similar to the gap between consumers and intention, expectation and reality can be polar opposites. Marketers aren't the only people who have a hard time predicting the future, but they also struggle to reconcile the usefulness of intent as a metric.

The idea that consumers are becoming more fickle or unpredictable, is arguably one of the most frequently used predictions in reports like the CMO Survey. To date this is not supported by facts. By contrast, Jeff Bezos, Amazon's founder and CEO, once mentioned that he was more interested in the things that would not change in the near future, as these were the things he would be able to build his business on. This is a universal truth underpinning investment, so I wonder why marketers don't look at non-change in this way. Instead, they often ignore the things that are stable and can be truly predicted. Bill Bernbach (of DDB fame) introduced the notion of the 'changing man'. But concentrating efforts on the changing man has led to an even more pronounced focus on the short-term use of metrics.

So, everything is different now, right? Not so. Sixty years of scientific research has consistently found that people's buying behaviour follows a very robust pattern. Over that time, not much has changed when it comes to buying. One of marketing's most fundamental findings is that every brand's customer base looks like a banana (technically, reverse J-shape distribution). Although he left the fruit out of his description, it was Andrew Ehrenberg who first described the distribution of a brand's buyers as a Negative Binomial Distribution (NBD). As you can see in the illustration, most buyers are on the left of the curve. These people will have only bought the brand once or, at most, just a few times during the time period measured. This is arguably the most important insight: a lot of people buy a little, and a few do buy a lot (but there are fewer of them). It is because of this distribution (and the statistical patterns that sit below it) that brand growth depends on adding more buyers and these already large groups of (very) light buyers buying even once more. Rather than attempting to increase loyalty of the already heavy buyers. Think about relative expandability.

This model of distribution (technically called the NBD-Dirichlet model of buyer distribution) shows that collectively, people's propensities to buy will not vary much. It is a reliable, descriptive and predictive model of consumer buying behaviour. So remember this, all brands follow the reverse

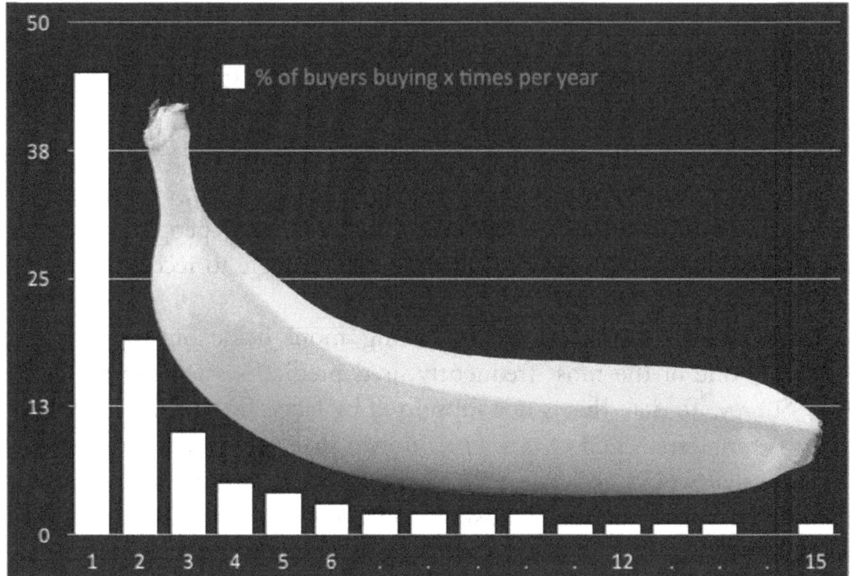

Fig. 1.1 The NBD and the banana

J-curve, with few people buying a lot and a lot of people buying a little (Fig. 1.1).

Bringing this back to how the marketing troops are currently faring, the nature of change in the media landscape means that marketers are often swimming against the current of science. Data and technology have only exacerbated this, and they find themselves focusing on what is more immediately and easily measurable.

Evidence of being on the wrong side of the banana is perhaps most famously connected to Peter Field and Les Binet. Their work on the IPA Effectiveness Awards Databank which contains results from thousands of campaigns from 1998 to 2016, shows that overall campaign effectiveness is declining. This is because companies who focus on activation and short-term objectives are targeting heavy buyers (or at least not fishing for light buyers as well). Targeting technology is set up for this. It tends to look for those who have bought before, and more rarely for those who haven't or who buy infrequently. Mostly because the infrequent buyers are harder to see. Activation campaigns aimed at existing buyers will give you instant rewards because they were likely to buy anyway, but not because the campaign was more effective. How many evaluations deduct *normal* sales without the campaign? Instant results like clicks and Likes mean instantly happy CMOs and CEOs. Peter Field rightly compares these activation campaigns to fireworks: a short-lived spectacle with little residue.

To me the notion of focusing on the changing man is like an industry driving backwards. I grew up in the Netherlands. In the 1980s a Dutch television show hosted backwards driving competitions on race circuits. Roughly translated, it was called *Racing in Reverse.* Some say that Dutch reverse racing is the funniest thing they have ever seen. Reverse gear is there for a reason in vehicles and is used only occasionally. If we want to move forward, we tend to use the other gears. Businesses aiming to grow, need to choose the forward gears and focus on lighter and non-buyers on the left-hand end of the banana. Even though we need to continue to encourage heavier buyers, focusing all of our efforts on the right-hand end of the banana is like driving in reverse.

1.2.3 The Wrap up

If you haven't noticed the degree of change in our world over the past 15–20 years, perhaps you have been living underground. While change is normal and healthy, learning how to navigate this new thing called cable TV after years of linear TV is in no way comparable to navigating this new thing called surveillance capitalism after years where our privacy and our data was largely protected. So at the risk of sounding cliché, the rate of disruption in our industry, and for the poor unsuspecting consumer, is like no other time in history. And this is not from a place of Factfulness, rather from a place of fact. This book aims to help marketers and advertisers shift into forward gear given the current state of play and act as an eye-opener in readiness for the future state of marketing.

MEANWHILE IN THE REAL WORLD

Scott Galloway the Prophet

One of the most revered, and certainly feared, commentators in our industry is Clinical Professor Scott Galloway (NYU Stern School of Business). He is revered because of his numerous high-profile board positions including Eddie Bauer, The New York Times Company, Gateway Computer (acquired by Acer) and others. Because he has founded and grown many companies, including: Prophet (a brand strategy firm), Red Envelope (a multichannel retailer that went public in 2002), and L2 (a subscription research and business intelligence firm that benchmarks the social, search, mobile, and site performance of the world's largest consumer and retail brands). L2 was acquired by Gartner for US$134 million in 2017.

But it's his no-holds-barred, no-mercy style commentary that makes him one of the most feared. Particularly by those he calls the Four Horseman: Amazon, Apple, Facebook and Google. In 2017, he discussed the 'hidden' DNA of these companies, talking about how Apple mimics religion with its own belief system, objects of veneration, cult following, and Christ figure. And how a disturbing aspect of today's media duopoly, Facebook and Google, is their abdication from being called media at all, which seems to absolve them of all social responsibility.

The public gut punches continue each week in his *No Mercy/No Malice* blog where he shares his take on tech and relationships in the digital economy. Titles like 'Billionaires Behaving Badly', 'Facebook 1, Congress 0', 'From Russia with Likes', 'Alexa, how can we kill brands?' and 'WeWTF' are sure to conjure fear from those he targets. Part of his blog includes his highly anticipated annual predictions on the happenings in the media and tech industry for the following year. Clearly, some are designed to get your attention, like the prediction that Sheryl Sandberg and MacKenzie Bezos will marry in 2019, but most are serious and based on his research. Looking back over the years Galloway gets his predictions right only about half of the time, but when he does get it right the tectonic plates of our marketplace shift just a little bit. He makes big calls about big industry players, here are a few that he got right:

- Slack will take over email for internal communications in 2016
- Netflix will become the operating system for television in 2017
- Cryptocurrency will crash in 2018
- Big tech firms will start to see bigger fines and tighter data protection laws in the EU and more hearings in the US in 2018
- Amazon to surpass Apple in value in 2018
- Voice (specifically Amazon's Alexa) is going to be the next big thing in 2018
- Walmart will become the online grocery leader in 2019
- weWork will not IPO in 2019 (well, they tried).

If his 2020 predictions are right, by 2020 Uber will lose 80% of its value, 30% of all searches will be 'queryless' as visual search becomes dominant and Amazon will be in the healthcare business. I'm not sure how I feel about an appointment with Dr. Amazon, we will have to wait and see.

Bibliography

ACCC. (2019). *Digital Platforms Inquiry* (Final Report). Canberra: Australian Competition and Consumer Commission.

ACCC. (2019, July 26). *Holistic, Dynamic Reforms Needed to Address the Dominance of Digital Platforms*. Media release.

Auletta, K. (2018). *Frenemies: The Epic Disruption of the Advertising Industry (and Why This Matters)*. New York: HarperCollins.

Baker, L. (2018). *Amazon's Search Engine Ranking Algorithm: What Marketers Need to Know*. Retrieved from https://www.searchenginejournal.com/amazon-search-engine-ranking-algorithm-explained/265173/#close.

Binet, L., & Field, P. (2007). *Marketing in the Era of Accountability: Marketing Practices and Metrics That Increase Profitability*. Henley-on-Thames: World Advertising Research Center.

Binet, L., & Field, P. (2013). *The Long and the Short of It: Balancing Short and Long-Term Marketing Strategies*. London: IPA.

Boches, E. (2014). Bill Bernbach and the Beginning. *Medium*. Retrieved from https://medium.com/what-do-you-want-to-know/bill-bernbach-and-the-beginning-7e49c2242390.

Booth, D. (2012, August 34). Is Avis 'Trying Hard' Enough with New Slogan? *CNBC*. Retrieved from https://www.cnbc.com/id/48859670.

Bothun, D., & Gross, D. (2016, June 7). Sir Martin Sorrell of WPP on Coming Together. *Strategy + Business*. Retrieved from https://www.strategy-business.com/article/Sir-Martin-Sorrell-of-WPP-on-Coming-Together.

Carlson, N. (2010, March 5). At Last—The Full Story of How Facebook Was Founded. *Business Insider*. Retrieved from https://www.businessinsider.com.au/how-facebook-was-founded-2010-3?r=US&IR=T#we-can-talk-about-that-after-i-get-all-the-basic-functionality-up-tomorrow-night-1.

The Economist. (2018). If Facebook Will Not Fix Itself, Will Congress? *The Economist*. Retrieved from https://www.economist.com/united-states/2018/04/11/if-facebook-will-not-fix-itself-will-congress.

Ehrenberg, A. S. C. (1959). The Pattern of Consumer Purchases. *Applied Statistics, 8*(1), 26–41.

Field, P. (2017, April 18). Peter Field: Short-Termism Is Killing Effectiveness. *Stuff (NZ)*. Retrieved from https://www.stuff.co.nz/business/91501478/peter-field-shorttermism-is-killing-effectiveness.

Fowler, E. (2019, July 26). The ACCC's 23 Recommendations to Fight Google, Facebook. *The Australian Financial Review*. Retrieved from https://www.afr.com/policy/economy/the-accc-s-23-recommendations-to-fight-google-facebook-20190717-p52874.

Galloway, S. (2019). *No Mercy/No Malice*. Retrieved from https://www.profgalloway.com/.

Gartner. (2019). *Daily Insights*. Retrieved from https://www.l2inc.com/daily-insights.

GlobeNewswire. (2019). Analysis on the Worldwide Car Rental Market 2019–2024—Avis Budget Group, Sixt, Hertz, Enterprise Holdings, and Europcar Group Are Dominating. *GlobeNewswire*. Retrieved from https://www.globenewswire.com/news-release/2019/06/20/1871913/0/en/Analysis-on-the-Worldwide-Car-Rental-Market-2019-2024-Avis-Budget-Group-Sixt-Hertz-Enterprise-Holdings-and-Europcar-Group-are-Dominating.html.

Goldstone, C. (2017, November 21). *Big Shoes to Fill*. CBC Media Forum Presentation, Vancouver.

Goodwin, T. (2018). *Digital Darwinism: Survival of the Fittest in the Age of Business Disruption*. London: Kogan.

Hoffman, R. (2018). *Blitzscaling: The Lightning-Fast Path to Building Massively Valuable Companies*. New York: HarperCollins.

McNamee, R. (2018). *Zucked: Waking Up to the Facebook Catastrophe*. London: Penguin Random House.

Neff, J. (2015). Former Mediacom CEO Alleges Widespread U.S. Agency 'Kickbacks'. *AdAge*. Retrieved from https://adage.com/article/agency-news/mediacom-ceo-mandel-skewers-agencies-incentives/297470.

Nelson-Field, K. (2013). *Viral Marketing: The Science of Sharing*. Melbourne, VIC: Oxford University Press.

Nelson-Field, K., Riebe, E., & Sharp, B. (2012). What's Not to "Like"? Can a Facebook Fanbase Give a Brand the Advertising Reach It Needs. *Journal of Advertising Research, 52*(2), 262–269.

Parekh, R. (2012, August 27). After 50 Years, Avis Drops Iconic 'We Try Harder' Tagline. *AdAge*. Retrieved from https://adage.com/article/news/50-years-avis-drops-iconic-harder-tagline/236887.

Pariser, E. (2011). *The Filter Bubble: What the Internet Is Hiding from You*. New York: Penguin Press.

Richards, K. (2017, July 24). How Avis Brilliantly Pioneered Underdog Advertising with 'We Try Harder'. *Adweek*. Retrieved from https://www.adweek.com/creativity/how-avis-brilliantly-pioneered-underdog-advertising-with-we-try-harder/.

Rosling, H., Rosling, A., & Rosling-Roennlund, A. (2018). *Factfulness: Ten Reasons We're Wrong About the World—And Why Things Are Better Than You Think*. London: Sceptre Books.

Snijders, W. (2018). *Eat Your Greens: Fact-Based Thinking to Improve the Health of Your Brand*. Kibworth, UK: Troubador Publishing.

Somers, J. (2017, March 21). The Like Button Ruined the Internet: How Engagement Made the Web a Less Engaging Place. *The Atlantic Boston*. Retrieved from https://www.theatlantic.com/technology/archive/2017/03/how-the-like-button-ruined-the-internet/519795/.

Williams, J. (2018). *Stand Out of Our Light: Freedom and Resistance in the Attention Economy*. Cambridge: Cambridge University Press.
Wu, T. (2016). *The Attention Merchants: The Epic Scramble to Get Inside Our Heads*. London: Atlantic Books.
Zuboff, S. (2018). *The Age of Surveillance Capitalism: The Fight for a Human Future at the New Frontier of Power*. London: Profile Books.

2

Recipe for Good Media Research

A numberwang is a statistic you can bandy around that sounds impressive but, with a bit of context, is less so.

Steve Weaver, Director of Research, Insights and Education, ThinkTV Australia

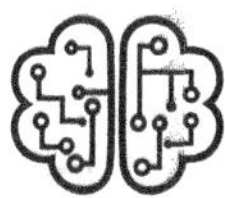

To explain how we operate here at Amplified Intelligence, and to help you navigate through the four million insight pieces published near daily in the trade press, I need to take you on a quick trip back to the first century BC. I promise to teleport you there and back with only the most relevant disruption to your thinking. And I might have exaggerated about the four million insight pieces, but rest assured we take our numbers very seriously. So seriously, I think it's important to pass on what we know about how to differentiate 'numberwang' from rigour, the guiding principles of good research to look for and those which we apply.

2.1 The Vitruvian Man

2.1.1 Rule-Based Systems

I have drawn up definite rules to enable you, by observing them, to have personal knowledge of the quality both of existing buildings and of those which are yet to be constructed.

Marcus Vitruvius Pollio, Preface, Book I (Morgan's translation)

K. Nelson-Field, *The Attention Economy and How Media Works*,
https://doi.org/10.1007/978-981-15-1540-8_2

Back in the first century BC, Marcus Vitruvius Pollio, a Roman civil engineer and architect (80–70 BC—after c.15 BC) knew exactly what good research looked like. Vitruvius is most well-known for his multi-volume work, *de Architectura libri decem,* which translates to *Ten Books on Architecture.* He is cited as the original classical authority on rule-based architectural systems and his works inspired the famous drawing by Leonardo da Vinci of the Vitruvian Man (the perfect specimen of a male body relative to the relationship between proportion and stable structure). Vitruvius suggested that the practice of architecture should be based on guiding rules and principles, both ideological and practical. Adhering to rules around Order, Arrangement, Eurythmy, Symmetry, Propriety and Economy, would prevent structures from 'falling to decay'. If an architect diligently follows these rules, 'durability will be assured'.

It was Vitruvius' goal to disseminate this knowledge, to transform these codifications from metaphysics to practice. *de Architectura* was hugely successful and Vitruvius' advice has been followed for centuries, with his work still included in first year foundation architecture courses at universities around the world.

2.1.2 The Vitruvius of Marketing

Introducing the Vitruvius of modern marketing—Andrew Ehrenberg (1926–2010). His highly awarded work in the 1950s and 1960s set the foundation for marketing rule-based systems today. Andrew Ehrenberg was a professor and a statistician who, for over half a century, contributed to marketing literature around systematic patterns in buyer behaviour. His main contribution was put forward as a collection of works with co-author, Gerald Goodhardt, in *The Dirichlet: A comprehensive Model of Buying Behaviour* (1984).

In essence, the NBD-Dirichlet model of consumer behaviour is a stationary, probabilistic model that has been shown to accurately describe how consumers behave and how brands perform across a very broad range of conditions. We introduced in Chapter 1 that Ehrenberg's discovery shows that a brand's customer base can accurately be described by a negative binomial distribution (NBD) of buying rates. Meaning, under most conditions the distribution reflects a high incidence of light buyers (shoppers who have a low to close-to-zero purchasing rate), fewer medium buyers, and very few heavy buyers. Despite the model being a stationary model (which tells us that brand growth is actually unusual and relatively hard to achieve), brands clearly do grow and decline over time. It tells us a great deal about how market share change occurs and what marketers can do to foster these rare movements.

The key point of Ehrenberg's work is that the path to growth is less of a marketer's choice, rather a statistical certainty. It turns out that marketing is less magic and a lot more science; not unlike the philosophy of Vitruvius many centuries earlier.

The two key generalisations from the model that shape the way we should undertake marketing and inform the methodological considerations behind media research, are Double Jeopardy and the Duplication of Purchase Laws:

The Law of Double Jeopardy describes the relationship between the size of a brand and the loyalty of its customer base. The Double Jeopardy pattern reflects the additional benefits of a brand's size. Not only does a big brand have more customers (penetration), but its customers are slightly more loyal than the customers of smaller competitor brands. Brand growth comes from larger movements in customer numbers and simultaneous, but far smaller, corresponding movements in the loyalty of those customers. So, for marketers that seek to grow, marketing efforts should be focused on attracting non/lighter brand buyers to the brand. This strategy will increase penetration rates rather than focus on increasing the loyalty of existing heavy-buying customers.

Duplication of Purchase Law describes the way in which competing brands share their customers. It shows that the proportion of customers that a brand shares with a competitor is dependent upon the size of that competitor. For example, Coke is the largest brand in the soft drink market and sees less sharing of customers with its competitors. While a much larger proportion of Dr Peppers customers (a small brand in the market) will also buy Coke. This phenomenon shows that customers consistently, and predictably, buy from a small group of brands, and one brand in this group (the largest brand) is favoured over the others.

Ehrenberg suggests that once these expectations are set, the implications for marketers become clear. Growth comes from getting more customers, not from attempting to increase loyalty; and customers are shared between brands in a systematic fashion. Regardless of any brand's unique selling proposition or image, the biggest potential for brand growth comes from getting the customers of the biggest brands in the category to try you at least once.

REMEMBER THIS SIMPLE TRUTH

Understanding the NBD-Dirichlet Model of Consumer Behaviour is vital to media planning as it allows us to define robust benchmarks for what can be expected from advertising.

2.1.3 The Litmus Test is Replication

If P reveals truth, then replication should reveal the same truth.

Geoff Cumming, Professor of Psychology, La Trobe University

Marketing moves at a fast pace. The late Bob Barocci (former President and CEO of the Advertising Research Foundation) once remarked that marketers were putting change ahead of learning. The same can be said for marketing researchers. With accelerated change comes accelerated learning and accelerated learning can carry error.

Let's step back a bit. In the empirical sciences, meaningful results come not from testing increasingly specific hypotheses, but building on existing results. A replication study tries to repeat an earlier study, using similar methods and under similar circumstances, to determine the reproducibility of the earlier study's results. Replication with extension is where a study is conducted using similar methods but with slightly varying circumstances, such as different countries, sample demographics or product categories. Replication (with extension) increases the likelihood that the results are valid, predictable and will hold over time and under fire. That is what makes them truly valuable. Replication is about looking for results that are reasonably similar, not significantly different. Significantly different results should ring alarm bells as they are often wrong.

REMEMBER THIS SIMPLE TRUTH

Replication is the key to rigorous research. When a result holds over a range of conditions, the result can then be used predictively.

It's easy to be caught up in the excitement of a significant finding. New findings are typically reported as being of statistical or managerial significance, and case studies seem to carry far more weight than they should. Increased pace and a monumental rate of change has prompted a willingness to accept the 'findings' of unregulated studies that 'sound reasonable'. Marketers under pressure to build sales growth on an unrelenting frontier, turn to the most influential advice or that which best fits with their plan so far. The result is a large amount of unsubstantiated marketing advice, taken as fact. Andrew Ehrenberg and John Bound (2000) themselves have this advice: 'We believe that the main stumbling block in developing law like relationships is that statistically minded researchers usually try to find an instant solution to a practical problem, without first investing in longer term R&D to establish what, if any, generalisable relationships exist in the data. This is like astronomers trying to predict the data of an eclipse without having studied the planets.'

REMEMBER THIS SIMPLE TRUTH

When a study is claiming a single instance breakthrough, sit and wait for a repeated result before changing course.

An example of 'research gone wild' can be found in psychology. A November 2019 article (www.nature.com) outlined a sector in crisis, suggesting that only half of all seminal studies published can be repeated. An international team of some 200 psychologists commissioned to replicate some of the biggest findings in their field found that key findings that have shaped our thinking on human behaviours, may not be real. These include the concepts of social priming, subliminal exposures and facial-feedback hypothesis, all of which have implications for marketing. The research team does call out the irony of their generalised finding that only half of all studies can be replicated, but the irony doesn't stop there.

The opening quote of this section by Professor Geoff Cumming, noted author on statistics reform and Emeritus Professor of Psychology at La Trobe University, suggests that the truth of the P score is in its replication. Cumming challenges the widely accepted belief that P scores of statistical significance demonstrate whether an effect is reliable and endurable. He's not alone, in 2016 American Statistical Association warned against the misuse of statistical significance and P values due to their potential to lead to false conclusions. Cumming shows that statistical significance can change, and change drastically, even when a random sample is drawn from the same data. The irony here is not from what he says, but that his field is psychology.

Reasons for replication failures can include anything from fluke or statistically weak findings, omission of outliers (data fraud), lack of controls and not considering the whole picture (unknown variables that influence study outcomes). Our own work on attention and media impact, from previous work including *Viral Marketing: The Science of Sharing*, highlights how lack of controls and failing to look at the bigger picture, directly and significantly impact the media sector.

For any new media, marketers seem to go through a worship stage. We have seen it with Facebook and Google Ads, and more recently with Instagram influencer marketing. In the worship stage, the excitement of possibilities shines all of the light on attractive positives leaving the reality of ugly truths in the shadows. The time it takes for successfully duplicated results just doesn't fit with the speed of uptake and the desperate need to be ahead of the pack. Of course, the ultimate result is that one-offs and case studies are claimed as laws. Before you know it, someone has written a bible based on a collection of rules that can't be replicated, and qualitative examinations of a single instance are being sold as truth. The excitement wanes around about the time sales start to decline and too much budget has been assigned.

So, as you consider the four million must-read insight pieces that come across your desk tomorrow (again perhaps a slight numberwang), consider whether their insights would last as long as Vitruvius or Ehrenberg's advice. It's the reason the generalisable NBD-Dirichlet model of consumer behaviour sits behind our research informing the questions we investigate, the methodological considerations (including experimental controls) we choose, and what we recommend.

However, just to make the Ehrenberg disciples twitch I would like to throw a contentious cat among the pigeons. Even Vitruvius would see variations to the foundational concept of stability when more modern materials became available in later centuries. So, in challenging boundary conditions the NBD-Dirichlet should be tested to understand the effect (if any) that the era of surveillance capitalism might have on the distributions and/or patterns. This is not to suggest it would (or it wouldn't) but changes in our industry, our human ability to process, our accessibility and the nature of supercomputers, have never in history been so fast and significant. It is vital we continue this study of consumer behaviour to understand the long-term effect on such foundational work. After all, the litmus test is replication and life would be boring without the ability to challenge.

REMEMBER THIS SIMPLE TRUTH

When things are vastly different than expected, be cautious, it usually means it's not right. Look for work that fails to decay.

2.2 The Good and the Ugly of Advertising Measurement

Combining shortening budget cycles and an abundance of bad research with the effortlessness of publishing on the www, creates a perfect storm for advertisers. In fairness, the academic process does move at a glacial pace, so waiting for double blind reviewed journal articles is no more helpful. Sneaking in through the murky light of this perfect storm is our old friend bias. Sometimes bias is created through non-independence and sometimes through methodological design. Non-independence or influence from interested parties is easier to notice, although sophisticated marketing can conceal financial and ideological bias. Bias through methodological design is a more insidious problem. Not all non-independent research is bad, but all poorly designed research is. Here are a few simple things to look out for in research design before you accept and apply new findings. After all, applying findings from poorly designed research can impact your media buying, badly.

2.2.1 Naturalness and Experimental Controls

Of all marketing activities, advertising impact is particularly difficult to research. One of the complications is 'naturalness'. True 'in-the-wild' advertising exposure, where a viewer is exposed to advertising in a completely natural setting, is gold standard. But it brings with it complications.

Natural advertising exposure means some people in the audience might see an ad once at 9 p.m. on a weeknight, while others see the ad five times across different times of the day and week. Some might be exposed to a highly emotive ad that has high attention pulling power, while others are exposed to less than stellar creative. Some might be exposed at a higher rate of viewability, while others are exposed to ads that are barely on screen (see Chapter 6); some might see the same ad many times, while others just once. An almost endless array of exposure options can occur, and the differing variables are all potentially influential in generating advertising impact, either on their own or combined.

So how do you know if it was the advertising that had an impact and not the environment in which the viewing took place? The answer is, experimental controls. The ability to control for, or isolate, one variable while the effect of the other is considered. And this control is vital, it can literally mean the difference between comparing apples with apples, and apples with pears. And when apples and pears are compared, the results can end badly (see Meanwhile in the Real World: Numberwang down under).

REMEMBER THIS SIMPLE TRUTH

Good research applies experimental controls that isolate real effect.

While controlled conditions are ideal in that they are better for measurement precision, the problem is that simply knowing you are in an experiment for advertising can fundamentally change your behaviour. Even with the most honourable intentions, people behave differently when it is obvious they are being watched or tested, generating 'reactive error' (i.e. responding to the experimental environment itself). The challenge has always been to apply experimental controls without trading off against a 'natural' viewing experience.

While content can be controlled and subsequent frequency or creative effects can be minimised in the laboratory, the un-naturalness of this environment brings with it its own bias. You might be on a couch in a laboratory, but it's not your couch or your family and not your typical interruptions (the kids, the cat, the doorbell). Sometimes just knowing you're being watched from behind the one-way glass can bias a result. Laboratory-based experiments also tend to have low generalisability because they rely on whatever sample of subjects the researcher can persuade to visit the lab. Often the cost of running experiments is high, financially limiting the sample in terms of numbers. This is particularly the case with much of the attention work using biometrics, such as electrocardiogram (heart rate) and functional magnetic resonance imaging (brain activity). Laboratory-based work tends to limit scaled replication.

If you are really lucky, you might be asked to wear some sci-fi fashionable gaze-tracking goggles. They are cheaper, making it easier to recruit larger samples. Granted, at least some of the newer versions of this hardware no longer have cables, so you can view programming at home without being connected to the mothership. But even though they more closely resemble heavy framed glasses, wearing goggles on your head is probably not typical of your standard at-home TV or internet session. This all becomes crucial if the research is designed to reveal a winner and a loser, such as cross-platform effectiveness.

As an example of this type of bias in market today, an (unnamed) media platform funded a study where viewers were asked to wear gaze-tracking goggles while viewing for 45 minutes on their platform, yet the viewing time for the (unnamed) competitor was 90 minutes. This raises two issues. Firstly, uncomfortable hardware will be more uncomfortable when tasked with wearing it for twice as long. So it is highly likely the participant was less distracted and uncomfortable (and paying more attention, which is the point of the study) at the 45-minute mark than the 90-minute mark. Secondly, to make matters worse this study considered the proportion of time in high/low levels of attention across the absolute period of time. So, (with the numbers changed slightly to maintain platform anonymity) 60% of 45 minutes (27 mins) is actually less in absolute time than 40% of 90 minutes (36 mins), but the story was sold that 60% attention is better than 40%. If that's not enough, after the study viewers were asked whether they agree or disagree that the number of ads during the session was annoying. The panel showed in favour of the funding platform—the one that showed the panel half the number of ads! While this experiment was in-home and somewhat natural (other than the goggles), the rest of the study showed bias in many areas which is (very) likely to have skewed the results.

The method applied must be consistent across all platforms. Too often we see 'winning' findings in trade-based insight pieces, only to discover that the methodologies used are vastly different across platforms. This makes them incomparable, or worse, clearly favouring one platform over another.

SUMMARY OF GOOD—Consistent methodology when comparing across platform. Natural viewing environment. Experimental controls for mediating variables. Scaled for generalisability.

SUMMARY OF UGLY—Allowing bias to alter the 'good' research fundamentals, introducing inconsistency, and allowing a funding partner to claim the win on the back of it.

REMEMBER THIS SIMPLE TRUTH

Look out for the uglies in research design, particularly in cross-platform effectiveness when the research is designed to demonstrate a winner and loser platform.

2.2.2 Market Share is the Forgotten Child

The complications of naturalness can extend into theoretical considerations. We know, for example, that advertising is noticed more by people who already buy (or more heavily buy) the advertised brand than by people who are light or non-buyers. Similarly, as previously noted, big brands have more buyers who buy slightly more often. So, without accounting for this in the analysis, any observed heightened attention or chance of buying could just simply reflect the brand's market share or a skew in the sample frame (towards heavier buyers), rather than the effectiveness of advertising.

The simple thing that can fix this is a baseline. Market share offers a baseline, but it is the forgotten child in research design. Using NBD-Dirichlet, a brand's size has more of an impact on how a consumer responds to advertising than the advertising itself. The need to incorporate the brand's size as a baseline becomes paramount to understanding the true value of any differences measured. Let's consider social metrics for a moment. Brands often default to soft engagement measures such as Likes, comments and shares as a measure of brand success. But the reality is big brands simply have more buyers who engage, which drives social metrics up, rather than the content necessarily being any more engaging. And the inverse is true. Lower Mental Availability (which is a symptom of being small) means that the ads of small brands are less likely to be recalled. This doesn't mean that all ad campaigns of small brands are ineffective, it simply means brand size hijacks the outcome when considered at an aggregate level. The same can be said here for brand lift studies and offline word-of-mouth. Brand lift studies experience other issues lurking below the surface, while offline word-of-mouth has been found to be more a function of audience size (in consideration of TV programs) than an over-abundance of program loyalty.

When studies fail to account for market share they run the risk of misattribution of effects. Without context, the findings might be inflating the importance of any differences. A big issue for our industry is that many commercial offerings, those that sell market research, could be completely misleading their client (hopefully unintentionally).

SUMMARY OF GOOD—Applying market share baselines when considering differences from one brand to another in any research capacity (i.e. pre-testing, recall, brand lift, sales, online engagement, mental availability, etc.).

SUMMARY OF UGLY—Market research companies that don't understand the nature of buyer behaviour and sell research that doesn't include brand usage baselines.

REMEMBER THIS SIMPLE TRUTH

Accounting for market share is an important factor when considering differences in advertising/media research. It can mean the difference between any result and the right result.

2.2.3 Beware the Legacy Proxy

Sales is the holy grail of business. If you don't sell stuff, you don't survive. Simple. And the importance of understanding the influence of advertising on sales is a no-brainer. The trouble is, distinguishing the influence of advertising on aggregated sales is often very difficult, near impossible. Marketers tend to revert to legacy measures, tested at the individual level, that have at some point assumed to resemble sales impact. In an attempt to solve issues surrounding proxies, academic researchers in the 1990s arrived at single-source data as the gold standard for measuring advertising effects. Single-source data involves collecting both natural advertising exposure and later buying behaviour from the same individual buyers over an extended period (typically up to a month after the exposure). Analysis of the data at a fundamental level involves comparing the buying behaviours of individuals who were exposed to advertising, with those who were not. This methodological approach eliminates many of the problems previously noted. But (and it's a big BUT) it is very expensive. A few global brand owners can afford it, and only a very small proportion of publicly available studies use this type of gold-standard data.

This is why proxies are used so abundantly in market. Single-source data is out of reach for most. Legacy measures are easy to collect and, well um, handed down by predecessors. That's the legacy part. A desire for consistency in measurement over time, coupled with low-cost collection, makes it hard for managers to change. Purchase intention and brand recall are the most commonly used. But advertisers are not the only ones who default to easy-to-collect proxies. We see big media use them too. Problem is, legacy measures don't typically reveal the truth.

Intention scales usually involve the self-reported probability of a buying event occurring. The difficulty with intention is that it's based on the ill-informed concept that advertising is highly persuasive and can force a sale. Underpinned by the ingrained AIDA Hierarchy of Effects model developed in 1898, this models suggests that advertising has to first make one aware (in a fully cognisant way), then interest comes, then product desire, followed by the sweet smell of action. In this scenario, intention is the proxy for action. It relies on the assumption that cognition affects behaviour. To compound the confusion, other versions of AIDA switch out awareness for attention. It then becomes: advertising must first secure attention, then hold it (interest), followed by the consumer passing through the hierarchical stages to action. The premise being, '...without attention, you can hardly persuade them of anything'. Yes, this is a quote from a large US management company called Changing Minds, dedicated to exactly that.

A critical flaw surfaces here—*awareness* and *attention* are not interchangeable! Awareness is about cognitive realisation, conscious understanding and grasp, but attention can also have an impact at lower levels of cognitive awareness. A viewer does not need to be fully aware and paying high, controlled, sustained attention for the ad to have an impact (see Chapter 5). In this regard, attention and awareness are very different constructs. That these terms are so flippantly switched, demonstrates a lack of theoretical understanding in regard to attention, AIDA and its action proxy.

There is plenty of evidence in the literature to show that intention significantly overstates behaviours, to the point where it may not be any better than mere chance. It is consistently reported that around only 50% of consumers who voiced an intent to buy actually follow up on it. Additionally, there is no consensus around whether the non-intenders or the intenders are more accurate in their response.

What is definitive though is that intention is correlated with previous buying. This means that an intender is much more likely to have previously bought the brand than a non-intender. Again, this goes back to the importance of baselines. Without understanding the baseline usage behaviour of the panel, the intention score recorded during in-market testing could simply reflect previous buying rather than the advertising having any great effect.

Recall is a measure of explicit memory where the consumer has to consciously think back to advertising exposure moments to retrieve from memory and report via recall and recognition tasks. Recall as a measure has been around since the 1950s. The original rationality for using it was the belief that recall is a necessary condition for a change in behaviour or attitude. Suggesting that the purpose of an ad is to persuade someone to buy, and that high levels of recall of the brand message means sales will surely follow. There is little to no evidence that a sale will follow, and given advertising is not persuasive, there is actually more evidence that it won't.

The point here comes back to accounting for previous buying behaviour. There is a well-established generalisation that users of a brand have a much higher propensity to recall (and pay attention to) advertising than non-users. In fact, users are around twice as likely to recall as non-users. When you couple this with not accounting for brand size, the recall study you just read (and made decisions upon) just got skewed. For example, big brands will have more existing users than small brands (fact of Double Jeopardy) that also recall more. So, without any baselines (both market share and controlling for users/non-users in the sample frame), the bigger brand will always report higher recall than the smaller brand. Rarely do proponents of recall apply such baselines.

Back in the real world, this becomes problematic for marketers when an insights team releases a study that shows that recall on Platform A is much higher than recall on Platform B. If the creative wasn't held constant, where the *same* ads were exposed over both platforms to the control and test groups, the inflated recall measure might simply be because the ads seen on

Platform A were generally bigger brands than those seen on the Platform B (and/or because the sample frame was skewed to heavier buyers).

Let's assume for a moment that the researcher or insights team has applied the appropriate baselines and/or controls. There is plenty of evidence to suggest that recall actually can be a useful metric for measuring explicit memory, BUT do not be fooled into thinking that it is a suitable proxy measure for all attention. It is not. And this is a really important point.

Okay, I hope you're still with me. Recall has been widely noted as a suitable proxy for high concentrated attention conditions, where the viewer is watching intently in a state of full consciousness. It is under these conditions that recall has the capability of measuring explicit memory of past experiences. It is also widely noted that such measures are valid only under these conditions and not in brand choice/retrieval situations where attention is divided. This means that recall is not suitable for measuring implicit memory where viewer attention is less concentrated and under the threshold of full consciousness.

Chapter 5 is dedicated to deepening our understanding of the many levels of attention and the relative states of consciousness, but for now here is the kicker. In the age of distraction, the larger majority of attention paid to advertising is at lower levels of processing than you think. But while high-attention processing is rare, low-attention processing does have an impact and that incidental ad exposure can actually influence consumer decisions and support the formation of consideration sets.

It's why I'm hammering this point home. Recall is being used as a proxy for measuring attention because it is easy and inexpensive. However, as a stand-alone measure it is not only reporting a small part of the story, it is wrongly changing the narrative (which is far worse). As an industry if we have any chance of driving the attention economy in the right direction we need to find a 'true north' measure.

SUMMARY OF GOOD—When recall is baselined properly it can identify high-attention processing.

SUMMARY OF UGLY—Intention is no better than chance, recall is ineffective for indirect or subconscious exposure given cognitive effort is required to be able to recall and retrieve memory.

REMEMBER THIS SIMPLE TRUTH

Be cautious of insight pieces that use measures of intention and recall. These proxies demonstrate a weak correlation to in-market sales performance.

2.2.4 Not All Machines are Like R2-D2

R2-D2, who is now inducted into the Robot Hall of Fame (yes, there is one), is unwavering in loyalty and indisputably reliable. His one job is to use ingenuity and intellect to save the galaxy and his humans—Luke, Leia and Han. Turns out that not all machines are like R2-D2. Just because something is tech, doesn't mean it should be trusted without question. Just ask Bob Hoffman, he has some pretty strong views on that. Some research technology on the surface appears to deliver magic, but underneath fails to address the complications and biases I've mentioned. In essence, it could be amazing technology, but poor construct. Or good construct, but poorly measured. Either of these combinations is bad.

Take Paul Ekman's emotions coding, for example, emotions as a construct is good to measure. Researchers have shown that the emotion triggered by an advertisement is important for its effectiveness. But questions have been raised over the use of commercially available emotion software development kits that use Ekman's six emotions as their measure.

Ekman conducted seminal research in the 1950s on the biological correlations of specific emotions to universal facial expressions. He found that a basic set of six facial expressions was linked to the same six emotions across five countries. He built an atlas of facial expressions (perfect for training data some 60 years later). These universal emotions are now commonly used in facial technology that considers advertising impact. They are: happiness, anger, sadness, disgust, surprise and fear. Of the many criticisms that have surfaced, one points out that Ekman's work really only found that there are some universal expressions across countries, not that these are the only emotions expressed. There are literally hundreds of papers that show a justified extension of Ekman's framework, adding in more emotions.

For the work behind *Viral marketing: The Science of Sharing,* we wrote our own emotions framework. It incorporated Ekman, but we did it because we believe that the Ekman 6 as a stand-alone framework is unbalanced. We used high and low arousal emotional pairs, evenly balanced by positive and negative valence. The point of my story is that it now looks as though emotions are not universal, after all. Yet, largely due to the training data available, the Ekman 6 emotions are still at the core of our advertising testing systems.

While not all robots are like R2-D2, they're not all out to kill us either. We can't let fear trap us in the dark ages. A high-profile academic institution recently published this on technology, 'Today's world of never-ending technological breakthroughs creates the illusion that jumping from bandwagon to bandwagon is moving forward, when we are really going around in circles.' That's like telling Thomas Edison to get off the electric light bandwagon after thousands of unsuccessful attempts. Just as well he was prepared to test and fail, otherwise I'd be writing this in the dark.

As much as any proud disruptor would like to think that they were solely responsible, it doesn't work like that. Most great breakthroughs don't come from an individual, they happen through the culmination of efforts by many people on the discovery trail. When you're looking for research technology you can trust, don't just check the person who put their name to it. Check for the crowd of people on whose shoulders their discovery stands. If you can find a solid, theoretically robust foundation, you're on the right track.

REMEMBER THIS SIMPLE TRUTH

Look for research technology that is based on solid foundations. It should be theoretically robust, transparent and evidence-based.

2.2.5 A Story About a New Approach to an Old Problem

A great deal of the material you will read in the coming chapters comes directly from our own extensive research on media effectiveness, viewability, attention and much more. Given I have just asked you to challenge the research you read, here is an open description of our methodology.

Let's start by saying the egg came first, not the chicken. What this means is that our own research framework (supported by bespoke technology) was built from the ground up to support the research questions we needed to answer. We did this to ensure that before we started measuring effectiveness (and attention), our measure was empirically led and would provide the right result, not just any result. As such, our system applies everything we know about the generalised laws of brand growth and consumer behaviour, yet incorporates technology and application that challenges the boundaries of research design. It is robust yet agile—an important distinction.

It all started with a question

Several years ago we were asked a research question. And then another. And another. The questions were about the impact that different media attributes have on consumer behaviour, specifically sales outcomes. The attributes have included: ad pixels, view time, device type, platform type, clutter, ad placement, sound and marketing context including dual screening, decay, frequency and others. Around about the same time, attention as an impact metric was moving its way from other disciplines onto the advertising agenda. A growing concern over inattention catapulted the study of attention from psychologists and economists into the advertising sphere. Now we were met with questions about attention and pixels, attention and view time, attention and programming, attention and clutter and many, many more. At the time of writing this, we have answered up to 200+ killer research questions, ×4 countries, ×9 platforms and 85,000 test ad views.

The ability to measure attention (at scale) changed everything. It allowed us to be more diagnostic at a second-by-second level so we could better understand 'why' rather than just 'what'. More excitingly, it meant that we could help pivot the entire research conversation around the appropriateness of attention as a proxy for sales and play a role in the trading future of our industry (see Chapter 5).

We had to build something bespoke

To answer these research questions, we would need individual level single-source data, with a twist. We needed a way to deliver a view, in a 100% natural environment, yet maintain experimental controls on test ads, across multiple platforms, across countries, across devices, while collecting attention, sales and viewability metrics. Simple right?

Fast forward to 2019 and this is how we collect research data and process it:

1. Customised app to collect the data

A key component of our research framework is a customised collection app that each research participant downloads onto their device. The app ensures the following process takes place (in chronological order):

a. It exposes the right viewer to the right viewing session (i.e. directs them to Facebook, YouTube, Twitter, TV channels or others). If it's Facebook, the respondent logs in using their own log-in details (which we don't scrape in case you're wondering), so that the Facebook experience appears completely natural. The viewing session time is aligned with the typical experience on the platform (but importantly we consider impact by average second, to remove any biases as previously mentioned).
b. As soon as the respondent is experiencing the platform, the app activates the user-facing camera/webcam when an ad is displayed on their screen. This collects facial footage at five frames per second, which is

then converted to binary data using one of our attention models. The model is altered for each device type used, so that screen information can be incorporated into the determination of where the face is looking on screen.

c. Where the research requires the viewer to be subject to test advertising material, on digital platforms the app is designed to intercept the natural ad load in real time and replace the ads they would have seen with a test ad. So instead of seeing an ad they were naturally meant to receive (i.e. via targeting), they will see our purpose-chosen test ads. Intercepting the advertising in this way ensures the ad viewing that does occur, closely matches the normal user experience, in that they would have naturally been served an ad in that position. This allows us to keep the creative constant across platforms and is crucial in order to accurately differentiate between platform performance differences and creative differences in advertising effectiveness, while also controlling for targeting nuances between platforms. In terms of the technology's capabilities, we can intercept ad loads for both video and static ads and can do so for any type of placement (i.e. mid-roll, pre-roll, in-feed). For linear TV, test advertising is edited into the content prior to the exposure occurring (more detail on linear TV below).
d. The app tags all ads the participant is exposed to, whether intercepted or in the wild. This is how we track the pixels of ads that are on screen, their duration on screen, the proportion of the screen that the ad covers as the viewer scrolls (we call this coverage), and whether the sound is on or off and how high the volume is.
e. After the viewing experience, the collection app redirects the participant to the virtual store that houses the choice tasks for each of the test brand categories. The respondent is asked to make a choice in each of the test brand categories from the test brand and several competitor brands (shown in random order). This is a validated approach for actual choice behaviour; experiments applying this method have long been undertaken in health, transport, economics and marketing. We use the method to reveal potential differences between exposure groups in overall behavioural preference for advertised brands.
f. Short Term Advertising Strength (STAS) is calculated after gathering choice from a viewer session. STAS is calculated by determining the proportion of category buyers who bought a specific brand having NOT been exposed to brand advertising (control group), and comparing it to the proportion of category buyers who WERE exposed to the same brand advertising (test group). By collecting buying data from a non-exposed

control group of participants we can differentiate between real advertising effects and the impact of brand size on buying propensity. This is a key differentiator to the many sales or brand lift studies in the market today. A STAS score of 100 indicates no advertising impact in that those who were exposed to the advertising were just as likely to purchase as those who were not. A score above 100 indicates that the advertising had a real incremental impact on sales.

g. Following questions of product choice, additional relevant information about the respondents is also gathered. That is, whether they are typical, heavy, or light users of the brands chosen and the test brand. All of these measures are used to triangulate with attention and product choice for greater validity. We also collect (via questioning, with permission) basic demographic information at this point.
h. Once the respondent has finished their session, the app becomes redundant on their device (please refer to our data privacy policy on amplified-intelligence.com.au).
i. Television collection varies slightly from online platforms. A second phone is set up in the home (using hardware we send them) which streams content to their TV and provides a user-facing camera. Participants can freely get up and leave as they normally would in a natural TV experience. This technology includes Adaptive Bitrate Streaming (like Netflix) to ensure people with average wi-fi can fulfil completion.

2. Machine Learning Model and Data Analytics Framework to process the data

The data we collect is then sent through our Data Analytics Framework, which incorporates custom machine learning models to transpose the recorded webcam footage to a second-by-second measure of attention. Early literature on attention to media (mostly in TV) talked about three types of attention—active watching, passive viewing and avoidance. This early literature (in the 2000s) sought to ethnographically understand where people were physically looking when TV advertising aired. The need for such consideration was grounded in the thoroughly sensible assumption that Peoplemeter panellists were probably not perfectly recording exactly how attentive they were being during their TV watching (i.e. measurement error associated with accurate pushing of the button was probably pervasive). Jump over to the psychology literature on attention and dual processing and similar levels of attention emerged based on three grades of consciousness processing (High, Semi, Sub) (see Chapter 5 for Attention Conceptual Framework).

Our output attention score is an average per second, based on the extent to which eyes were on screen and on the advertisement (connected to a pixel reference point via an ad tag). Average second is the most relevant comparison where advertising varies in length. In particular, we consider:

1. **Active Attention**: Was the respondent looking directly at the ad?
2. **Passive Attention**: Was the respondent in eye shot, but not directly looking at the ad?
3. **Non-Attention**: Had the respondent walked away from the TV, or completely looked away from the mobile screen during the ad-frame?

Our models are also trained for device orientation, remembering, of course, that people flip their phones around depending on what they're viewing. Much of the gaze literature talks about the main factors that any technique should possess to guarantee good measurement as being: (a) accuracy, (b) reliability, (c) robustness, (d) non-intrusiveness, (e) free head movements, and (f) real-time response. These are the factors we strive for.

Finally, all data, including all viewability metrics, and other attributes such as sound and brand choice, is then matched at the individual view level. Voilà questions answered. Well not quite, this is where the humans step in for comprehensive interpretation of the results. No computer can do that, yet.

2.2.6 The Wrap up

Marketers of today have it tougher than ever before, there are too many ways things can go terribly wrong. Is our system perfect? No. Do we continually strive for improvements? Yes. We do know that our system has been disruptive for its time and that we have managed to answer research questions robustly where many have failed. And we are proud that we brought a little bit of R2-D2 back to the future by way of ingenuity and empirically-led intellect. Remember, always scratch below the surface when investing in systems and research that can have a fundamental impact on your business. And always ask the question, which came first the chicken or the egg?

MEANWHILE IN THE REAL WORLD

Numberwang down under

There's no doubt that numbers are slippery. Intentional and accidental numerwangs are the reason our industry is teetering on a sinking raft of bad measures. In August 2019 in Australia, Facebook felt the full wrath of a numberwang.

In conjunction with global professional services company Pricewaterhouse-Coopers (PwC), they produced a report about media consumption in Australia. Called *My Screens: Video Consumption in Australia,* it made some bold claims about 'unique audience'. The fun started when Facebook announced on Australian trade press site AdNews that it's, 'Time to rethink consumption assumptions'.

In this instance Facebook was right, it is time to rethink consumption assumptions, BUT we need to be crystal clear on what lies beneath our measures. Within 48 hours another big player, Nielsen, had challenged their numbers and the report vanished like a bursting bubble.

At the heart of the numberwang were exceedingly high Facebook audience numbers. Always the first clue: when something is very different from what you would expect then it's time to re-check numbers and method. In this case, according to Nielsen, online text consumption data was incorrectly used in place of video consumption data. But the result fitted beautifully with what Facebook was hoping for, showing them to be the top performing media platform in Australia.

The numberwang: According to the published study, Facebook dominates the Australian media landscape, reaching 17.3 million 'unique audience' members per month. On top of this, PwC calculated (using a supporting Nielsen dataset) that users spend 882 minutes with video per month on the platform.

The reality (also from Nielsen data): Facebook's true monthly video audience is 4.5 million, and that doesn't include mobile, the device primarily used to access the platform. This makes the engagement time with video on Facebook 79.5 minutes per month.

For this numberwang, the data were correct, but they belonged to another discussion.

Bibliography

Amrhein, V., Greenland, S., & McShane, B. (2019, March 20). Scientists Rise Up Against Statistical Significance. *Readers Digest*. Retrieved from https://www.nature.com/articles/d41586-019-00857-9.

Armstrong, J. S. (1985). Long-Range Forecasting: From Crystal Ball to Computer (2nd ed.). New York: Wiley.

Bartlett, T. (2013, January 30). Power of Suggestions. *The Chronicle*. Retrieved from https://www.chronicle.com/article/Power-of-Suggestion/136907/.

Beattie, A. E., & Mitchell, A. A. (1985). The Relationship Between Advertising Recall and Persuasion: An Experimental Invetigation. In L. F. Alwitt & A. A. Mitchell (Eds.), *Psychological Process and Advertising Effects*. London: Larence Erlbaum Associates.

Bird, M., & Ehrenberg, A. S. C. (1966). Intentions-to-Buy and Claimed Brand Usage. *Operational Research Society, 17*(1), 27–46.

Chandon, P., Morwitz, V. G., & Reinartz, W. J. (2005). Do Intentions Really Predict Behavior? Self-Generated Validity Effects in Survey Research. *Journal of Marketing, 69*(2), 1–14.

Cumming, G. (2012). *Understanding the New Statistics: Effect Sizes, Confidence Intervals, and Meta-Analysis*. New York: Routledge.

Davis, D., Golicic, S., Boerstler, C., Choi, S., & Oh, H. (2013). Does Marketing Research Suffer from Methods Myopia? *Journal of Business Research, 66*(9), 1245–1250.

Ehrenberg, A. S. C. (1959). The Pattern of Consumer Purchases. *Applied Statistics, 8*(1), 26–41.

Ehrenberg, A. S. C. (1988). *Repeat-Buying: Facts, Theory and Applications*. London: Oxford University Press.

Ehrenberg, A. S. C. (1993). Even the Social Sciences Have Laws. *Nature, 365*(30), 385.

Ehrenberg, A. S. C., & Bound, J. A. (2000). Turning Data into Knowledge. In Chuck Chakrapani (Ed.), *Marketing Research: State of the Art Perspectives: Handbook of the American Marketing Association and the Professional Market Research Society*. Chicago, IL: American Marketing Association.

Firth-Godbehere, R. (2018, Septemer 6). Silicon Valley Thinks Everyone Feels the Six Emotions. *How We Get to Next*. Retrieved from https://howwegettonext.com/silicon-valley-thinks-everyone-feels-the-same-six-emotions-38354a0ef3d7.

Furr, N. (2011, June 9). How Failure Taught Edison to Repeatedly Innovate. *Forbes*. Retrieved from https://www.forbes.com/sites/nathanfurr/2011/06/09/how-failure-taught-edison-to-repeatedly-innovate/.

Goodhardt, G. J., Ehrenberg A. S. C., & Chatfield, C. (1984). The Dirichlet: A Comprehensive Model of Buyer Behaviour. *Journal of the Royal Statistical Society. Series A (General), 147*(5), 621–655.

Harrison, F. (2013). Digging Deeper Down into the Empirical Generalization of Brand Recall Adding Owned and Earned Media to Paid-Media Touchpoints. *Journal of the Advertising Research, 53*(2), 181–185.

Jarrett, J. (2016, September 1). No Reason to Smile—Another Modern Psychology Classic Has Failed to Replicate. *Readers Digest*. Retrieved from https://digest.bps.org.uk/2016/09/01/no-reason-to-smile-another-modern-psychology-classic-has-failed-to-replicate/.

Kennedy, R., & Northover, H. (2016). How to Use Neuromeasures to Make Better Advertising Decisions: Questions Practitioners Should Ask Vendors and Research Priorities for Scholars. *Journal of Advertising Research, 56*(2), 183–192.

Levine, M., Morgan, G., Hepenstall, N., North, N., & Smith, G. (2001). Single Source for Increased Advertising Productivity in a Multimedia World. In *Advertising Research Foundation Workshop*. Chicago, IL: Advertising Research Foundation.

Mason, M., & Tadros, E. (2019, July 30). PwC Accused of Using Wrong Nielsen Numbers. *Australian Financial Review*. Retrieved from https://www.afr.com/companies/media-and-marketing/pwc-accused-of-using-wrong-nielsen-numbers-20190729-p52brq.

McIntyre, P. (2019, July 30). Gravy Train: PwC's Facebook Storm Last Week, KPMG This Week with ThinkTV? *Mi3*. Retrieved from https://www.mi-3.com.au/29-07-2019/gravy-train-pwcs-facebook-storm-was-last-week-kpmgs-turn-week-thinktv.

Mele, M. L., & Federici, S. (2012). A Psychotechnological Review on Eye-Tracking Systems: Towards User Experience. *Disability and Rehabilitation: Assistive Technology, 7*(4), 261–281.

Morgan, G., Levine, M., & Dorofeev, S. (2001). A New Method to Measure Media Casualness for Magazines and Newspapers. In *10th Worldwide Readership Research Symposium* (pp. 185–204). Venice, Italy.

Morwitz, V. G., & Fitzsimons, G. J. (1999). The Mere-Measurement Effect: Why Does Measuring Intentions Change Actual Behavior? *Journal of Consumer Psychology, 14*(2), 64–74.

Morwitz, V. G., Steckel, J. H., & Gupta, A. (2007). When Do Purchase Intentions Predict Sales? *International Journal of Forecasting, 23*, 347–364.

Namias, J. (1959). Intentions to Purchase Compared with Actual Purchases of Household Durables. *Journal of Marketing, 24*(1), 26–30.

Nelson-Field, K. (2013). *Viral Marketing: The Science of Sharing*. London: Oxford University Press.

Nelson-Field, K., & Riebe, E. (2017, September). How Advertising Attracts Attention. *ADMAP*, 19–21.

Nelson-Field, K., Riebe, E., & Sharp, B. (2013). More Mutter About Clutter: Extending Empirical Generalizations to Facebook. *Journal of Advertising Research, 53*(2), 186.

Newstead, K., Taylor, J., Kennedy, R., & Sharp, B. (2009). The Total Long-Term Sales Effects of Advertising: Lessons from Single Source. *Journal of Advertising Research, 49*(2), 207–210.
Northover, H. (2012). *Assessing the Value of Neurophysiological Measurement for Advertising Pre-testing. Are Biometrics Better?* (Unpublished PhD thesis). University of South Australia.
Patterson, R. (1997). What Vitruvius Said. *The Journal of Architecture, 2*(4), 355–373.
Pollio, M. V. (1960). *The Ten Books on Architecture* (Morris Hicky Morgan, Trans.). New York: Dover Publications.
Romaniuk, J. (2012). Are You Ready for the Next Big Thing? New Media Is Dead! Long Live New Media! *Journal of Advertising Research, 52*(4), 397–399.
Sharp, A., & Riebe, E. (2000). *Examining the Accuracy of Probability Scales in Social Issues Research*. Institution Griffith University. 1139–1143.
Sinfield, D. Facebook. (2019, July 22). Video Killed TV's Starring Role: Time to Rethink Consumption Assumptions. *AdNews*. Retrieved from http://www.adnews.com.au/opinion/video-killed-tv-s-starring-role-time-to-rethink-consumption-assumptions.
Strong, E. K. (1925). *The Psychology of Selling and Advertising*. New York: McGraw-Hill.
Tadros, E. (2019, July 29). Australians Distrust Facebook More Than ASIO on AI. *Australian Financial Review*. Retrieved from https://www.afr.com/technology/australians-distrust-facebook-more-than-asio-on-ai-20190729-p52bqt.
Teixeira, T. (2014). *The Rising Cost of Consumer Attention: Why You Should Care, and What You Can Do About It* (Harvard Business School Working Paper No. 14-055).
Weaver, S. (2019, July 24). Warning: Numberwanging May Cause Blindness. *AdNews*. Retrieved from https://www.adnews.com.au/opinion/warning-numberwanging-may-cause-blindness.
Wilson. A. (2013, October 13). Social Priming: Of Course It Only Kind of Works. *Psychology Today*. Retrieved from https://www.psychologytoday.com/au/blog/cognition-without-borders/201310/social-priming-course-it-only-kind-works.
Wind, Y. (2008). A Plan to Invent the Marketing We Need Today. *MIT Sloan Management Review, 49*(4), 21–28.
Wind, Y., Sharp, B., & Nelson-Field, K. (2013). Empirical Generalizations: New Laws for Digital Marketing: How Advertising Research Must Change. *Journal of Advertising Research, 53*(2), 175–180.
Yong, E. (2018). Psychology's Replication Crisis Is Running Out of Excuses. *The Atlantic*. Retrieved from https://www.theatlantic.com/science/archive/2018/11/psychologys-replication-crisis-real/576223/.
Zinn, W., & Liu, P. C. (2008). A Comparison of Actual and Intended Consumer Behavior in Response to Retail Stockouts. *Journal of Business Logistics, 29*(2), 141–159.

3

How Advertising Works (so far)

Trying to understand the media without understanding advertising and marketing, its fuel supply, is like trying to understand the auto industry without regard to fuel costs.

Ken Auletta, Author, Frenemies

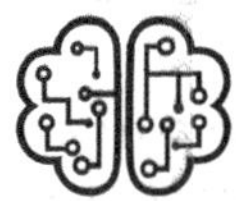

3.1 The Bert and Ernie of Marketing

At its simplest, there are two primary aspects to making decisions around marketing communication: the message (what to say and how to say it) and the distribution (where to say it and to whom). These two don't operate in a vacuum, like peanut butter and jelly, Bert and Ernie, macaroni and cheese, they are inextricably linked. How a marketer thinks advertising works directly shapes what is created, which media is chosen, who is targeted and what is measured.

It's almost a trick of the light that marketers think advertising is responsible for so much. Advertising is generally treated with disdain by the wider population, but many industry professionals are in love with the idea that we are in love with advertising and the brands that produce it. Thankfully, research over the years has eroded some previously held notions about how advertising works and marketers are slowly moving away from the belief that advertising is highly persuasive and immediate. This outdated understanding

K. Nelson-Field, *The Attention Economy and How Media Works*,
https://doi.org/10.1007/978-981-15-1540-8_3

is replaced with the knowledge that the impacts of advertising are commonly more subtle, take time to play out, and in turn, are difficult to measure. But we can't relax just yet. For every journal paper that proves (again) that advertising doesn't shift mountains, there are ten text books being distributed to the next generation of marketers, paying homage to the AIDA customer decision process as the holy grail. The reality is, that advertising has always worked in the same way regardless of our level of understanding. It's just our interpretation of the reasons for success that has developed over time.

So it's best to put our cards on the table now and briefly outline the guiding principles we align to on how advertising works. This chapter is not meant to be a long and exhaustive source of curated references on all things brand growth, there are other books on the market for that. It offers a layman's overview of the guiding philosophy that informs everything we do from how we collect data, to the technology we develop, to the narrative we deliver.

3.2 The Guiding Philosophy

3.2.1 Advertising Doesn't Persuade

The assumption that advertising equals persuasion is so ingrained in the USA that to challenge it elicits much the same reaction as questioning your partner's parentage.

Tim Ambler, London Business School

Imagine for a moment that advertising is the Arc de Triomphe. Unless of course you are French and find even this brief visualisation too unpalatable. While it's generally accepted that advertising must eventually drive sales, the debate around how advertising works lies in all the theoretically possible roads for getting there. Initially, the vast majority of practitioners believed that advertising worked by persuading audiences to believe in the brand and this would be enough to prompt them to buy. It was assumed that successful advertising campaigns would need to produce an observable and large change in buyer behaviour. When few examples of wholesale behaviour change achieving a massive uplift in sales could actually be produced, the theory was disproven.

The dominant theory back in the 1960s was that advertising was capable of persuading a non-buyer to change their behaviour to become a buyer. The final destination, rather than the path to getting there, was all that mattered. We now know that the impacts of advertising are not an immediately felt behavioural change, rather a subtler nudging of buying propensities across the market. Very successful advertising in the large part reinforces, rather than changes, behaviour. And this occurs over a long timeframe. Sure, there will always be a few oddballs in the audience who see an ad and just have to have that product then and there. But these outliers are never going to be a source for notable changes in aggregate sales levels. The more substantive impact of advertising is a small shift across the whole audience felt over time as buyers come into the buying window. And because each buyer comes into the buying window in their own time (rather than a substantial amount of people at once), an immediate effect will not be evident.

3.2.2 Advertising Impact is Small but Positive

In addition to the foundation work described by the generalisations from the NBD-Dirichlet, research around advertising and pricing elasticities provides an indication of the direction and scale of the returns expected. An elasticity is a ratio metric. For example, an advertising elasticity is the proportional uplift in sales impact results for every 1% shift in advertising spend. Pricing elasticities are always negative (i.e. a price drop generates a sales increase) and relatively large (a large sales increase for a small price reduction). Advertising elasticities are positive and comparatively small; that is, a large increase in advertising spend is required to generate even a small increase in immediate sales.

This means that brand growth (and decline) is a rarity and that advertising does not necessarily need to drive a large uplift in market share to be deemed successful. Advertising works to announce to potential buyers that the brand exists and then regularly reminds them of its existence so that when they are ready to buy from that category, the brand might come to mind. It moves advertising far away from the famous AIDA concept to one of awareness-trial-repeat (ATR), where awareness is more publicity based (general noticing) than seeking to change how people think and feel about the brand on the spot. This means that trial is less about a 'successful sales conversion' and more about an opportunity to be tested for future suitability. In communication, it's the difference between aggressive and assertive.

In advertising, we must accept that publicity, not persuasion, is how advertising works and that advertising makes its main contribution by building memory structures so that when a buyer is in market the brand might come to mind. We must also accept that *mere* market share maintenance, versus going backwards, is actually a considerable achievement.

REMEMBER THIS SIMPLE TRUTH

Advertising does work, it just doesn't cause the great seismic shift in mass buyer behaviour that marketers might think (or hope).

3.3 How Publicity Can Be Measured

3.3.1 What is Mental Availability?

If advertising doesn't shift mountains, and it can't be seen in aggregated sales, how can it be measured? There are two ways advertisers can directly understand the impact of advertising. One is single-source data which involves collecting both viewing behaviour and buying behaviour from the same individual over an extended period of time. But as noted in Chapter 2, it is expensive which limits its use to the global brands that can afford it. The other way is by tracking a brand's Mental Availability. This is not looking at sales, rather it considers whether advertising has had some impact on consumer memory (even if a sale is not evident).

Professor Jenni Romaniuk, the leading academic in this space, classifies *Mental Availability* as the strength (uniqueness) and prevalence (number of people) of the brand name and linked associations in a consumer's memory. Linked associations, if the advertiser has done their job correctly, act as cues that bring their brand to the surface of memory on different occasions, such as Coke and summer, De Beers diamonds and engagement, and here in Australia, Vegemite and breakfast. The more unique these associations are to your brand, the more likely the consumer will think of your brand over your competitor at the buying occasion.

Mental Availability has nothing to do with building brand love, intention to buy or any other proxy loyalty type measure. It is the simple notion of strengthening memory cues so that when you propose to your sweetheart on an Australian beach in summer as the sun rises, you think of stocking your picnic basket with cans of Coke, Vegemite and toast, and a thumping great De Beers diamond.

3.3.2 Why does it Matter?

Being considered at the time of product purchase, versus not at all, has obvious implications on sales. A brand with strong Mental Availability is more likely to grow, at least not decline.

Of course, a caveat to the above is that the brand is physically available to buy. If a brand is out of stock or hard to access, a customer will choose your nearest competitor with little thought (because we are loyal to switching not loyal to one). Just one reason that marketing and operations need to talk to each other. There's no joy in doing all of that advertising work only to have your nearest competitor scoop the sale.

In terms of measuring, Mental Availability is commonly both misunderstood and misrepresented. It is often passed off in brand research as brand awareness, consideration, brand personality or likelihood/intent of buying. But these are poor proxies and don't capture the underlying construct of Mental Availability nor do they account for market share baselines (as discussed in Chapter 2).

Advertisers who use these measures run the risk of wasting money on trackers that tell them little.

REMEMBER THIS SIMPLE TRUTH

Mental Availability is considered a market-based asset. Maintaining and building it should be considered a key objective of advertising.

3.4 Staying True to You

3.4.1 Becoming Unhinged with Differentiation

We're all special in our mother's eyes, but sadly that's where it ends. When it comes to the specific creative elements that help link buying cues to a brand, being special isn't worth it. Seeking differentiation via a unique selling proposition (USP) simply results in keeping your brand small because it completely unhinges any attempt to build strong Mental Availability.

Let's take a step back. Traditional product differentiation strategies (Rosser Reeves c.1940s) are based on the notion that product advertising should offer a unique benefit over its competitors to survive. Proponents of persuasion argue this is a necessary component of successful advertising because a strong differentiated proposition convinces the masses to buy one brand over the other.

A classic example of this is FedEx, 'When it absolutely, positively has to be there overnight' (1978–1983). FedEx was the first company to specialise in overnight air freight and first to implement package tracking. These were processes and service delivery that were undoubtedly the best of their time, so it's not surprising FedEx used them as the basis of their core slogan. The slogan was only prevalent for five years but ask any 40+ year old and I'd bet they could still associate it with FedEx.

Research has shown there are two underlying issues with attempting to differentiate. First is that the proposition has to be something the competition categorically cannot, does not, or can never offer. It must be real, totally unique and timeless. That is a hard call, most real product differences can be replicated. There are now many more companies than FedEx that express deliver goods overnight. As soon as the proposition is replicated, it breaks/blurs any memory links the original brand paid a lot of money to establish. Very few USPs are unique to one brand.

This leads us to the second issue: research consistently shows that consumers don't consider brands to be very different. Like we said, no-one is really that special. When we think back to our earlier discussion on NBD-Dirichlet norms, this is why consumers are polygamously loyal to a select few brands in the category. Even the most successful brand can be easily substituted with a competitor. The simple (and brutal) truth is that even a brand's heaviest users don't see them as that different from other brands available to them. Seeking to be different, even if it were possible to achieve, will deliver brand decline before it delivers any success.

Looping back into FedEx, their current campaign has nothing to do with the speed of service delivery or ability to track packages. Again, not surprising as even non-logistics companies like Amazon can compete in this space. Their overarching mission statement is 'Solutions powered by people', but this is not at the forefront of their advertising campaigns. Their individual campaign themes vary from year to year. In 2018, the campaign was called 'What we deliver by delivering'. Its proposition is that FedEx, above all their competitors, can deliver such things as comfort, memories, opportunity and joy.

The series of really lovely heartwarming ads, including a child who leaves her beloved toy at a motel, or a young man who receives a photograph album with treasured memories, did not offer a proposition of 'real' difference. Although pity the creative director that needed to follow in the footsteps of 'When it absolutely, positively has to be there overnight'. The point being, the campaign didn't need to show a point of difference to be successful.

REMEMBER THIS SIMPLE TRUTH

Seeking to be differentiated via a unique selling proposition (USP) will keep your brand small, and completely unhinge any attempt to build strong Mental Availability.

3.4.2 What is a Distinctive Asset?

So how can a brand build Mental Availability if selling propositions are ineffective? The answer is far simpler than most creative directors would admit. Making the brand distinctive is known to build memory structures and drive Mental Availability.

Distinctive brand assets are things that strongly tie the brand in the memory of most consumers. These can be creative elements: logos (Swoosh), colours (Cadbury Purple), fonts (Coke typeface), shapes (VW Beetle), slogans (Finger lickin' good), characters (Rich Uncle Pennybags) or they can be auditory elements, such as a jingle (Stuck on Band-Aid). As soon as you say 'Finger lickin' good' you know who this is for and your brain likely switches to their equally famous character with a white beard and moustache. The greater number of Distinctive Assets your brand has, the stronger and wider the footprint in memory.

Be warned, using them in the background or as an afterthought in advertising does not make them an asset. To be considered a Distinctive Asset, an element needs to evoke the brand (and only that brand) without prompting, for close to 100% of consumers, close to 100% of the time. This is not a five-minute job, nor for the faint-hearted. It takes time, unwavering commitment and money. The Distinctive Assets we have mentioned have been established over many decades, longer than the tenure of most CMOs.

Harland David Sanders has been dead for close to 40 years, but his brand legacy will never be forgotten. And this is exactly what he intended.

REMEMBER THIS SIMPLE TRUTH

Distinctive Assets are the glue between your brand and your customer's memory. Build and protect them at all costs.

3.4.3 The Wrap up

In finishing this chapter we need to go back to the beginning—to the title in fact. Marketing science, without a shadow of a doubt, has brought clarity to how Bert and Ernie work as a team. How the message and its delivery best maximise the opportunity for brand growth. However, following science we must also acknowledge the opportunity for conditions to change and for new findings to emerge. Which is why the chapter is called 'How Advertising Works (so far)'. For the now, the materials of marketing architecture haven't changed enough to cause colossal change in buyer behaviour patterns, so all of our work is underpinned by these patterns. But the next 10 years is gearing up to be the most disruptive in history. Again, just ask our futurists in Chapter 9. All researchers of marketing should keep an open mind, even if that makes them twitch.

MEANWHILE IN THE REAL WORLD

Colonel Sanders is bringing sexy back

KFC and their agency Wieden + Kennedy Portland have brought sexy to the brand. They have reinvented the image of the once wholesome and rather portly Colonel as a Chickendale (think of The Chippendales), a main character for a romance novel (Tender Wings of Desire), a buffed, tattooed and scantily clad virtual influencer and a dating game paramour.

They have been experimenting with the Colonel asset for a while. In 2017, they released for sale in time for Cyber Monday the KFC's igloo Faraday cage complete with the Colonel on top. That year also saw Billy Zane played a fully metallic Golden Colonel promoting the honey mustard BBQ flavour. In 2018, KFC livestreamed four hours of cats climbing on a Colonel Sanders cat scratcher (with 700,000 people tuned in), he also appeared as a limited edition large inflatable pool float, and we saw the first female Colonel played by country music star Reba McEntire.

KFC as an overall brand have never shied away from bold PR stunts. In 2016, KFC customers in Hong Kong were introduced to edible, chicken-flavoured nail polish. In 2017, KFC New Zealand offered chocolate truffles made to taste like spicy chicken marinade and the Colonel's secret spices. And, of course, during the famous UK chicken crisis in 2018, KFC took out full page ads to apologise for running out of chicken, using a simple but clever re-shuffle of their branding. They sent the internet spinning with—FCK.

But is making the once traditionally wholesome mascot into a sex symbol going too far? Or is it a clever way to extend an ageing Distinctive Asset to appeal to a younger audience? It's no different to other popular assets that have changed drastically over time like Louie the Fly, The Michelin Man, Ronald McDonald and Australia's own Bundy Bear.

The editor of AdWeek interviewed Andrea Zahumensky, CMO of KFC US where she argued that, 'Colonel Sanders has always been sexy, but our strategy is to find new, interesting and provocative ways to make Colonel Sanders a part of culture'.

Seeing Colonel Sanders dance around half naked in a video was certainly provocative. And it ticks the *unexpectedness* box, and the *unwavering commitment* box, so perhaps they are onto something.

Bibliography

Ambler, T. (2000). Persuasion, Pride and Prejudice: How Ads Work. *International Journal of Advertising, 19*(3), 219–315.

Bartiromo, M. (2017, November 24). KFC Offering 10k 'Internet Escape Pod' Ahead of Cyber Monday. *Fox News.* Retrieved from https://www.foxnews.com/food-drink/kfcs-most-outrageous-marketing-stunts.

BBDO New York. (2018). FedEx: What We Deliver by Delivering. *The Drum.* Retrieved from https://www.thedrum.com/creative-works/project/bbdo-new-york-fedex-what-we-deliver-delivering.

Culp, L. (2018, April 4). KFC's Most Outrageous Marketing Stunts. *Fox News.* Retrieved from https://www.foxnews.com/food-drink/kfc-offering-10k-internet-escape-pod-ahead-of-cyber-Monday.

Deabler, A. (2018, May 24). KFC Debuts Colonel Sanders Pool Float. *Fox News.* Retrieved from https://www.foxnews.com/food-drink/kfc-debuts-colonel-sanders-pool-float.

Ehrenberg, A., Barnard, N., Kennedy, R., & Bloom, H. (2002). Brand Advertising as Creative Publicity. *Journal of Advertising Research, 42*(4), 7–18.

Ehrenberg, A. S. C. (1988). *Repeat-Buying: Facts, Theory and Applications* (2nd ed.). Edward Arnold, UK: Oxford University Press.

Griner, D. (2019, September 12). A Brief History of Sexy Colonel Sanders. *AdWeek.* Retrieved from https://www.adweek.com/creativity/a-brief-history-of-sexy-colonel-sanders/.

Romaniuk, J. (2018). *Building Distinctive Brand Assets.* New York: Oxford University Press.

Strong, E. K. (1925). *The Psychology of Selling and Advertising.* New York: McGraw-Hill Book.

Wijaya, B. S. (2012). The Development of Hierarchy of Effects Model in Advertising. *International Research Journal of Business Studies, 5*(1), 73–85.

Wohl, J. (2017, January 30). Billy Zane is KFC's New 'Gold' Colonel. *AdAge.* Retrieved from https://adage.com/creativity/work/georgia-gold/50719?.

Wright, M. (2009). A New Theorem for Optimizing the Advertising Budget. *Journal of Advertising Research, 49*(2), 164–169.

Zanger, D. (2018, July 18). KFC Livestreamed 4 Hours of Cats Climbing on Colonel Sanders, and 700,000 People Tuned In. *AdWeek.* Retrieved from https://www.adweek.com/creativity/kfc-livestreamed-4-hours-of-cats-climbing-on-colonel-sanders-and-70000-people-tuned-in/.

4

The Evolution of Media Buying

Find ballplayers, not those who look good in baseball caps.

Tom Monahan, CEB

It would seem more appropriate for an actual buyer of media to write this chapter than a media researcher. Someone who actually plays ball. As such, this chapter is co-authored by Stuart Bailey and Schalk van der Sandt, both from PHD Media Australia. Stuart and Schalk take a brief look at the changes in media that led to the programmatic media buying we see today. They discuss how marketers can wield new capabilities in a way that adheres to the brand growth principles, proven through marketing science and research. Most importantly, they provide some juicy tactical advice at the end on how to navigate the new normal in privacy.

4.1 A Brief History of Media Buying

Few marketing related quotes have resonated through the ages as loudly as the oft repeated classic attributed to nineteenth century retailer, John Wanamaker, who allegedly joked: 'Half the money I spend on advertising is wasted; the trouble is I don't know which half.' The implication is that a significant proportion of media dollars spent deliver no impact, and given the

K. Nelson-Field, *The Attention Economy and How Media Works*,
https://doi.org/10.1007/978-981-15-1540-8_4

right measurement and targeting capability, this inefficiency could be eliminated. What a dream!

It's no surprise then that as the digital era technology heralded capability far beyond any that Wanamaker could ever have imagined, marketers across the globe became hopeful that a solution to this particular puzzle may well be within reach. It's an ideal that has propelled digital advertising investment beyond that of television to over US$200 billion in around 25 years (www.magnaglobal.com). The promise was perfectly demonstrated in a *New York Times* article back in 1999, where the founders of DoubleClick were profiled. Then President of DoubleClick International, Barry Salzman, who went on to be Google's first Head of Media, used the Wanamaker 'money half-wasted' joke as a way of describing the power of this new platform and added that, 'Thanks to Kevin O'Connor, co-founder and CEO of DoubleClick, no one's laughing anymore, at least not in the online world'.

However, almost 25 years on from the historic launch of the DoubleClick platform no marketer could honestly suggest that we've completely conquered the riddle. There may well have been some headway in unravelling the mystery, but the journey has obviously not been as clear cut as first thought. In fact, the investments we think offer the most value could very well be the biggest waste!

As most reasonable marketers would attest, there is no silver bullet to achieving success, however, certain principles do hold true despite major shifts in media consumption and technology trends. It's easy to be seduced by the siren song of tools and technology. However, without an understanding of these fundamental principles and the framework they offer, marketers often end up with counter-productive outcomes. The most prominent of these outcomes include: over-segmented audiences, quantity-over-quality media decisions, and a general misunderstanding of what to expect from your media.

Does this mean that we should disregard the advancements that have been made? Certainly not. But it does suggest that we should have a far more considered approach in the planning and application of digital media, to ensure that potential strengths do not become vulnerabilities.

REMEMBER THIS SIMPLE TRUTH

Don't be seduced by the siren song of tools and technology. Ensure a considered approach in the planning and application of digital media, or potential strengths may become vulnerabilities.

4.1.1 The Early Years

To understand the challenges brought on by digital developments, we need to understand the history of the digital media buying landscape, and the primary driving motivations behind the ongoing development of the ecosystem—audience, measurement and targeting. These elements have existed in various guises throughout the vast history of media, influenced largely by the dominant media of the period, technological capability, and consumer preference.

In Fig. 4.1 we see the first press ad in 1704 signals the start of our journey. This era spans through to the advent of the TV rating systems in the middle of the twentieth century. It was a period marked by large-scale mass media, large formats and panel-based measurement. It saw the development of modern press, TV, radio and out-of-home (OOH) into established mediums, and welcomed in measurement institutions like the Audit Bureau of Circulation and Nielsen. Sponsorship and fixed placement media were the order of the day and TV was starting to make its mark, stealing share, both attention and spend, from the more established media channels.

4.1.2 The Middle Years: Demographics Become the New Kid on the Block

Our leap into the next period, seen in Fig. 4.2, is marked by revolutionary innovation from the ABC TV network, which would go on to help shape the industry. A smaller player in a big market, ABC decided to champion their stronger demographics in an effort to differentiate and steal share from their bigger rivals. This was an early precursor to the use of advertising efficiencies as marketers could use panel-based data to target, buy and optimise their spend to a specific demographic rather than mass audience buys. In the

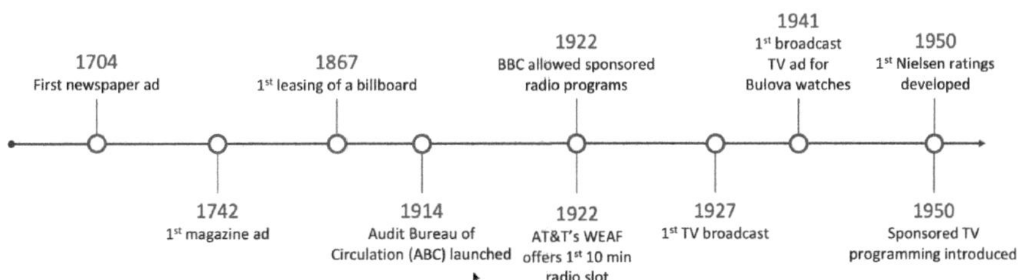

Fig. 4.1 The early years 1704–1950

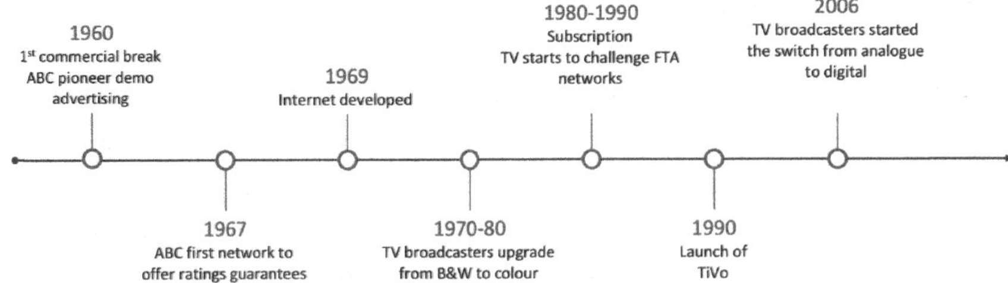

Fig. 4.2 The middle years 1950–1990

distant background a giant was emerging, but marketers wouldn't realise the game-changing potential of the internet for at least another 20 years.

Moore's law was in full effect and technology advanced at a rapid rate. Television, now the dominant player, was the main beneficiary of these advancements, evolving from black and white to colour, analogue to digital and from appointment-only viewing to on-demand through recordable boxes like TiVo.

4.1.3 The Later Years: A Giant Emerges

This brings us to the digital era shown in Fig. 4.3. Starting in 1990, media and marketing would be disrupted long before disrupting became fashionable. Panel-based demographic buying saw its biggest challenger in three decades—the world wide web and digital audience buying. During this period of 17 years we witnessed the birth of digital advertising, global power houses like Google, Yahoo! and Facebook, and the establishment of technology and measurement platforms.

In this era, technology and buying practices offered measurement that revolved around actual audiences and individual ad delivery, rather than the more established demographic and panel-based approach. We saw a proliferation of channels that started with search and display on desktops

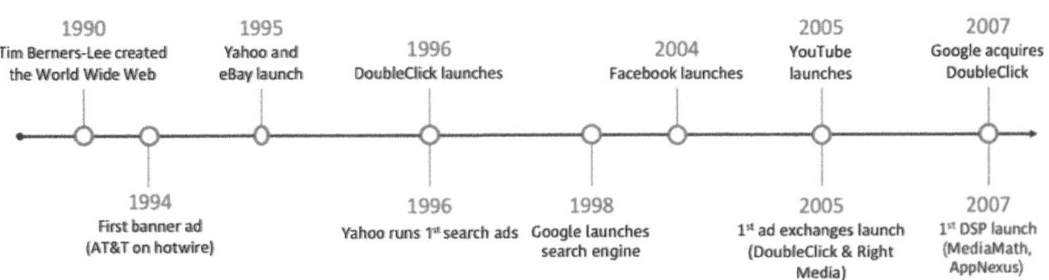

Fig. 4.3 The later years 1990–2007

through to the advent of social and e-commerce across mobile devices and tablets. This proliferation has transformed what used to be a niche bolt-on to the wider media plan into the sprawling ecosystem it is today. In fact, if we look more recently, and closer to home, between 2005 and 2018, digital ad revenue in Australia grew from A$488 million to A$8.8 billion (IAB 2005, 2018), accounting for more than 50% of total media spend.

There's no doubt that fragmentation, inconsistent buying currency, measurement challenges and under-regulation of the sector in this era has led to major complexity. But it has provided us with something that continually evolves, is driven by wide-scale adoption and innovation, and is actively shaped by consumer behaviour. Our new advertising reality is a moving target that has evolved past 2007; what we see now is an evolution occurring within the ecosystem that launched during this time.

4.2 Tech Changed Everything

4.2.1 We've Lost Control

While audiences could always choose whether to look at an OOH ad, read a print publication or watch a TV show, there were standardised ways to communicate with them, at scale, and in environments that were controlled. The internet shattered this paradigm. It brought a plethora of channels, platforms, sites and technologies online. The ability to reach a mass audience in a controlled environment started to fade.

The current digital buying ecosystem might seem unnecessarily complex. It is extremely crowded and it can be convoluted, but it's worth remembering that it is a system that has evolved to adapt to a massively fragmented consumer landscape.

Consider for a moment that in 2005, the year in which YouTube launched, there were close to 65 million websites on the internet and just over a billion internet users globally. Almost 15 years later this number has rocketed to just shy of 2 billion websites, and over 4 billion users, with penetration rates in developed regions of more than 80% (International Telecommunications Union 2017).

The explosion of content providers (some focusing on niche interests or catering to specific attitudes) and access unhindered by geographic or physical distribution limitations had two profound effects on the marketing world:

a. Search engines (after a challenging period pre-Google) eventually replaced directories as the preferred method of navigating information on the web. This would later manifest in a single, almost universal, gateway to the web, and a critical point of engagement for brands.
b. Audiences splintered into countless fragments becoming increasingly hard to reach online with single media buys. This led directly to the technology-driven buying environment we have today.

Through either tremendous foresight, sheer luck, or a combination of the two, a single company has come to dominate both aspects in the modern environment. Google has built a search engine that is largely unchallenged for scale in the western world, followed by its video platform, YouTube, now billed as the second biggest search engine.

On the second effect, Google's AdWords laid out the blueprint for what we call programmatic media today. It was a single, user-managed interface to manage biddable media buys in search, and later, banner ads across a massive global network of sites through AdSense. Outside of the Google environment though, buying of fragmented audiences was originally *simplified* by ad networks. These networks sold inventory on behalf of smaller websites, often many thousands of them looking to monetise their properties, or larger sites supplementing the efforts of their internal sales teams.

Hygiene metrics, as we know them today, were not the priority they are now, and these networks suffered from a lack of transparency. The exact placement of the ads was not known to the advertiser in most cases, so they were billed 'blind buys' or 'blind networks'. They survived though, thriving even, because they built technology that helped drive results, especially in the performance marketing space. Some would argue that this technology took advantage of a fundamental flaw in the digital marketing tracking ecosystem. This would later be validated through advances in viewability technology and digital attribution, which would show that many claimed sales were from ads that weren't viewed or didn't impact the path to purchase.

4.2.2 The Link Between Cookies and Golf

The simple browser cookie shifted priorities in the makeup of a digital target audience. Enhanced tracking capability, initially driven through ad server technology and later through Data Management Platforms (DMPs) and analytics platforms, meant that audience journeys were recorded. Segmentation could now be developed on browsing behaviour. Interest could be signalled and captured, rather than inferred through legacy category relationships with different demographics.

Behavioural segments could also be targeted all over the web, rather than only when they were active in the contextually relevant environment. No longer would golf enthusiasts only be contextually targeted on pages related to golf content. They could now be reached on pages completely unrelated to the topic, targeted by virtue of their past indication of golf enthusiasm.

Demographic profiles were swapped for behavioural or psychographic profiles, allowing targeting on abstract attributes, such as interest, affinity or attitudes, rather than the less informative age and gender criteria. At first this was only available across inventory within ring-fenced environments such as large publishers, but this soon developed into wider platforms and ad networks.

This ability to target beyond demographics and look at not only contextual but behaviour targeting across a large-scale audience, created a short-term fix to the scale conundrum of digital targeting. In the early days of the world wide web advertisers had to rely on large portals and destinations to target audiences, much like legacy media targeting. This new ability to find, categorise and target large audiences outside of contextual relevance meant that advertisers could scale these audiences in a way not achievable in the past.

As with so many of the early developments in the targeting space this was driven by players who could drive a more efficient sales outcome for clients. Although we know today that many of these 'sales' were not true sales and were either misattributed, double counted or based on ads that were never viewed.

Between 2005 and 2007 we saw the first ad exchange; first demand side platform (DSP) and the purchase of DoubleClick by Google. This created a disintermediation of media, with the media agencies and big tech platforms taking centre stage.

4.2.3 Programmatic Trading was Born

The likes of Google and Facebook, who had closed platforms and a wealth of data that over time has become even more closed off, rose to prominence. The ad networks who leveraged technology over inventory, that they didn't own or have exclusivity to, started to falter as more and more advertisers became cannier to trends like attribution, viewability, ad fraud and brand safety. Only the strongest would survive in a time of rapid consolidation.

Again, this evolution was largely driven by direct response clients in the first instance. There has been much written and documented around transparency and some of the practices within the programmatic period. The truth is there has been some misuse over time and there has also been immense progress made. At its best, programmatic is about giving control, transparency and performance back to advertisers but this has to be underpinned by trust, education and results.

What programmatic did do, from a targeting perspective, is to start a journey that enabled the advertiser to be closer to their data. This was later picked up by various other technology solutions like Data Management Platforms and has now created the multibillion-dollar Martech industry that is dominated by the likes of Adobe and Salesforce.

They have allowed advertisers to better organise, activate and measure their CRM and first party data, from their owned and earned assets, as well as their bought media. Which means that advertisers have been able to leverage their audiences more effectively across the consumer journey. This is where some of the earliest audience and data tactics and techniques started to come to the fore. Things like suppression of audiences who had already purchased a product, personalisation of the message and journey, cross-selling and building look-a-like audiences who share key attributes with high value customers, to name a few.

Programmatic media gives us the ability to efficiently target niche audiences with personalised messages within tightly defined parameters. This is helpful in situations where your target audience is narrow. One could argue that broadcast probably isn't always the best way to target IT business decision-makers, at least not at the lower end of the funnel. It's also a great solution to vary messages between distinct segments within a broader target audience, offering greater appeal and relevance to audiences, based on their targeting attributes. It is also true, however, that brands who have broad target audiences, like 'all category buyers', who consistently target niche audiences with sales focused offers will likely see a negative effect on brand health metrics, and ultimately sales volumes.

This split, and statements like one recently trumpeted in trade media that, '...programmatic doesn't work', are extremely unhelpful. It pits marketers on two sides of a fatally flawed premise: that the failure of the media to deliver against its objectives is somehow attributable to the way in which it was traded. The truth is that as with every other media channel, if the execution is not fit for the objective, then obviously the result will be sub-optimal. If programmatic isn't working for you, then most likely it is not the correct media to achieve the objective. Or perhaps it has not been executed well, or the objective has been misidentified. Either way, the failure is not that of the technology or underlying programmatic concepts. The machine will only do what you ask it to—so ask the right questions and monitor.

REMEMBER THIS SIMPLE TRUTH

When it comes to programmatic, the machine will only do what you ask it to. Ask the right questions and monitor.

4.2.4 Measurement Became a Science

Even though advertisers had more targeting options than ever, an attempt to combat the fragmentation of the digital audience saw the consolidation of buying through only a few platforms owned by an increasingly smaller number of massive global players. This has led to a major issue in the measurement space. When the big players like Google, Apple and Facebook make changes to their platforms, suddenly decades of work can become redundant. Systems built on cookies crumble as the big web browsers make them obsolete. Digital attribution models become defunct as Facebook and Google further retrench their data back into their platforms without any need to give reason or notice.

Where advertisers had previously relied on panel data to determine the likely makeup of audiences and project the reach numbers, digital technology has allowed for the precise measurement and reporting across every individual dimension of campaigns: site, placement, format and creative, amongst others. In terms of media metrics, there was a major leap forward for what advertisers could access:

- Impression volumes and click volumes offered precise indications of how far placements have spread, and how audiences have reacted to them.
- Digital capability allowed tracking and reporting of actions and the specific media which preceded it—essentially facilitating what is today referred to as last-touch attribution.

New media metrics provided an opportunity for advertisers to demonstrate, using technology and specialised metrics, the impact and return on marketing budgets. A welcome development which offered a more evidence-based justification for increased marketing spend. Return on Investment (ROI), Return on Ad Spend (ROAS) and 'cost per' metrics became the currency of success for many advertisers. The lower the 'cost per sale' of a placement or channel, the greater the proportion of the overall budget it could justify.

Efficiency became the bedrock of optimisation, kicking off a cycle of development that ultimately spawned entire sub-industries.

- *Analytics*: The introduction of web analytics programs allowed advertisers to analyse visitor behaviour across web assets, giving access to data on bounce rates, time on site, funnel drop-off rates and other factors that informed landing page conversion rate and site-user experience optimisation.
- *Attribution*: Multi-touch attribution models were developed to evaluate the contribution of media touchpoints that occurred prior to the last touch. They mainly covered digital advertising touchpoints and conversions but have in some cases been expanded to online-to-offline, and offline-to-online cross-channel attribution efforts.
- *Quality and accountability*: Hygiene metrics and measurement tools were developed with a focus on media quality, offering insight into previously unmeasurable aspects of media, such as the percentage of ad impressions of a placement that were viewed within the browser, the number of impressions that were served in unsuitable environments, or placements that were served by fraudulent actors.
- *Data management*: With the proliferation of mobile and smart devices, the ability to track behaviour across devices became critical; major platforms introduced the concept of tracking using an identity graph as opposed to a simple browser-based cookie identifier. An identity graph is a database that stores all identifiers that correlate with individual users. With the proliferation of devices, it helps advertisers understand if they are talking to the same person, whether they are interacting through their mobile phone, tablet or laptop. Advertisers have followed, creating this single customer view, through smarter use of data management and customer data platforms, to manage their own data assets to ensure they have as complete a view of their customers as possible.

The sheer wealth of data available and the constantly evolving landscape, has meant that measurement of digital activity is in fact infinitely more complex than so called, traditional channels. The truth remains that to excel and succeed in measurement in the digital age you need to continually invest in a scientifically robust and replicable measurement framework that ladders up to enduring business objectives. And it needs to be done on an ongoing basis with results analysed and checked against actual business performance.

Measurement is for life not just for Christmas sales.

REMEMBER THIS SIMPLE TRUTH

To excel and succeed in measurement in the digital age you need to continually invest in a scientifically robust and replicable measurement framework that ladders up to enduring business objectives.

4.3 The Future in a Private World

4.3.1 Serious Consideration

Most are still coming to grips with the new reality of everything we have discussed. The knock-on effect it has had on the traditional landscape has not gone unnoticed by governments and regulators. This book is spotted with discussion on the GDPR, the ACCC, senate inquires, anti-trust probes and more. Here are our thoughts on what happens next. The first thing to understand is that consumers and advertisers are not likely to use the internet any less. Secondly, even though we've seen an uptake in ad-free paid content there will always need to be a free ad-funded internet. Privacy challenges will have to be addressed, and when we consider the implications of privacy, a few trends start to emerge which require some serious consideration:

- *Local legislations have global implications*

As we've seen with GDPR, local law has global reach. Many major platforms and brands across the globe have ensured that they have the infrastructure in place to service EU audiences within the prescribed framework, whether the user is in the EU or in the US, Asia or Africa. We believe that further regulation will continue to govern how audiences within a jurisdiction are managed, regardless of where the communication is served from or where the audience is based. To ensure compliance, many of the major players will adopt the strictest possible standard to roll out globally. Global platforms/advertisers will end up adopting parts of GDPR, parts of ACCC and parts of the California Consumer Privacy Act.

We have already seen the likes of Google and Facebook retrenching their data, making it harder for advertisers to measure their campaigns holistically (be that attribution, brand metrics, etc.). In the short to medium-term this will continue and will strengthen their position in market until viable alternatives are found.

– *Consolidation will continue and data co-ops will emerge*

In order to compete with these behemoths, we're likely to see a lot more consolidation of local traditional media networks. They are increasingly realising the scale required to offer competitive customer intelligence, targeting, and reach products means joining forces with complementary businesses. In Australia, we have already seen the Nine and Fairfax merger, as well as the out-of-home consolidation with APN and JCDecaux, and OOH!media and AdShel. These sorts of consolidations enable operational efficiencies, greater scale in market and, specifically for the digital players, the ability to merge large and rich consumer data sets to try and offer a viable walled-garden alternative.

Marketing technology providers will also continue to go through a process of consolidation through acquisition and development, to provide advertisers with a single, end-to-end customer communications solution. This will limit the number of customer data 'handovers' between platforms, and the associated compliance watchouts. Again, we have already seen this to a large degree with Adobe buying Omniture, Tube Mogul & Marketo; Salesforce buying Datorama, Tableau, Krux; AT&T buying Time Warner, DirecTV and AppNexus, and; Amazon buying Sizmek.

We shouldn't be surprised if data co-ops become much more prevalent in the next 5–10 years. The large marketing technologies and big agency holding groups have already been developing them as possible alternatives for advertisers to reduce their reliance on the walled gardens.

– *The continued rise of subscriptions service*

Consumers for their part will continue to wrestle with the new value exchange. However, we're likely to see more affluent (and therefore premium) audiences increasingly opt for privacy over costs by choosing the ad-free experiences that many content providers are offering on a subscription basis.

We are already seeing the likes of Disney make a play in the subscription space with Disney Plus. They now own, or have majority share in ABC, Hulu, FX, National Geographic, ESPN, Marvel, Pixar, Lucas Films and 21st Century Fox. To put this into perspective, in the film market for the first half of 2019 they accounted for 45% of total global box office sales!

With consumers, especially young affluent ones, advertisers will need to focus much more on the value exchange. It will no longer be as simple as just capturing a customer's data and then using that to power their single customer view. In the future, brands need to give them a reason why they should be allowed to retain that data for future use. As a by-product we expect to see significant spend increases in channels offering ad-funded content and that still hold consumers' engagement, such as search, social, display, and out stream video media.

– *Advertisers building their own data ecosystems*

Lastly, we should expect to see more advertisers building premium ecosystems and value propositions themselves. We have seen this for many years with airlines and retailers and loyalty schemes but we can expect this to go further outside of the direct-to-consumer, retail and airline category.

It will increasingly be hard for brands to build, retain and activate consumer data sets. Regardless of the channel of delivery one of the biggest challenges will be identifying the consumer and ensuring that consent is given to store and use their data. In a world in which cookies no longer offer the same tracking and targeting functionality, we will have to rely on much more robust identity graphs, with persistent identifiers like device IDs, emails, mobile phone numbers etc.

These graphs will be developed by brands from their own customer bases, in a controlled and regulated manner, and utilised for segmentation and activation. Insights from these segments will be utilised to devise communication strategies for behavioural cohorts, and act as descriptive 'seeds' for audience development across the larger graphs of major media networks. This is where we will see the data co-ops playing a big role as they help build, enhance and activate these audiences across multiple environments, in a regulatory compliant manner.

4.3.2 So, What to do?

In summary, it seems that over the next few years, we can expect that the use of data for marketing purposes will get harder, which makes it critical for every organisation to have a data strategy in place. Marketing programs which have access to and use information more effectively are bound to be more successful. As these eventualities are realised, the gap will widen between those that have gradually developed and adjusted their data strategy according to market dynamics, and those that have not.

To make sure advertisers don't find themselves on the wrong side of the ravine, there are a few critical steps to consider:

1. Understand the role of data in your organisation, and how it can relate to media and marketing. This does not mean that you need to build massive databases and lists. Data can be descriptive or actionable, so yes, think about how you can create actionable segments, but don't forget to think about how you can use data to learn.
2. Know what 'good' would look like for your organisation. Your ambition does not need to be to achieve the ultimate hyper-personalisation engine. In fact, we need to move away from the ideal of known-individual granularity in targeting and delivery. Based on trends in both privacy legislation and technology, we're unlikely to see this kind of capability in the short to medium-term. 'Good' should be when you can employ technology and data to more effectively and efficiently deliver on your media strategy.
3. Build a team with the required capability and vision to deliver and further develop a data strategy. Understand that a programmatic platform can only deliver based on the instructions it has been given. Without people who understand the capability and limitations of platforms, the extent to which data can be utilised, and how to properly define the inventory criteria for optimum quality, you have nothing more than a blunt instrument.
4. Ensure that you have a technological infrastructure set up to action accordingly. This may require some help from experts! Not all platforms offer the same capability, and not all platforms work well with each other. Very few people would know the ins and outs of every piece of technology, so balancing best-in-breed capability with interoperability can be tricky.
5. Enhance your capability with strategic data partnerships. Try to broaden your understanding of your customers beyond the behaviours you can see in your own environment. How do they interact with other categories or media?
6. This all must be underpinned by the need to view media and marketing through a lens of science and theory. A good approach here is to develop a set of 5–10 marketing or advertising principles based on science best practice. Ensure that all your efforts, digital or otherwise, serve your principles.
7. Most importantly, ensure that you're measuring appropriately to observe both short and long-term business impact, and use your learnings to inform future planning.

REMEMBER THIS SIMPLE TRUTH

Understand the role of data, build a capable team and infrastructure. But most importantly understand the difference between short and long-term business impact.

4.3.3 The Wrap up

In a very real sense, we have a reversal of the well-known fable of the boiling frog. Unlike the frog who jumped out of boiling water only to die in a slowly boiling pan, advertisers, who wait until the pan is boiling to jump in and do not immerse themselves in the changing landscape will be far more likely to become extinct.

Change will be the only constant and those who try, fail and learn will be far better off than those who wait for the answers to come to them.

MEANWHILE IN THE REAL WORLD

The scientific method: Richard Dawkins

Question time at any 'in conversation' event can get interesting, but this one at the fourth annual Oxford Universities Think Week event, takes the crown. It was filmed at the Sheldonian Theatre, Oxford, on Friday 15th February 2013 and is well worth a watch on YouTube.

Questioner: The question is about the nature of science evidence. You both said, and I think most people here would agree with you, that we're justified in holding a belief if there's evidence for it or if there are logical arguments we can find that support it. But it seems like this in itself is a belief which would require some form of evidence. If so, I'm wondering what you think would count as evidence in favour of that and if not how do we justify choosing that heuristic without appealing to the same standard that we're trying to justify.

Dawkins: So…how do we justify, as it were, faith that science will give us the truth—is that the…?

Audience member (interrupting): How do we justify the scientific method?

Dawkins: Yes, um…it works. It works. Planes fly, cars drive, computers compute. If you base medicine on science you cure people, if you base the design of planes on science they fly, if you base the design of rockets on science they reach the moon. It works……(moderate pause)…bitches.

Bibliography

Dawkins, R. (2013). *Richard Dawkins—Science Works Bitches!* [Video file]. Retrieved from https://www.youtube.com/watch?v=0OtFSDKrq88.

IAB Australia. (2005). *IAB Australia: Six Months Ended June 2005* (Report). Retrieved from https://www.iabaustralia.com.au/research-and-resources/advertising-expenditure/item/11-advertising-expenditure/120-iab-australia-six-months-ended-june-2005.

IAB Australia. (2018). *Online Advertising Expenditure Report—Quarter Ended June 2018 (FY 18)* (Report). Retrieved from https://www.iabaustralia.com.au/research-and-resources/advertising-expenditure/item/11-advertising-expenditure/2625-online-advertising-expenditure-report-quarter-ended-june-2018-fy-18.

International Telecommunications Union. (2017). *ICT Facts and Figures 2017.* Retrieved from https://www.itu.int/en/ITU-D/Statistics/Documents/facts/ICTFacts Figures2017.pdf.

Internet Live Stats. (2019). *The Total Number of Websites.* Retrieved from http://www.internetlivestats.com/total-number-of-websites/.

Malik, D. (2019). Global Ad-Blocking Behaviors in 2019—Stats & Consumer Trends (Infographic). *Digital Information World.* Retrieved from https://www.digitalinformationworld.com/2019/04/global-ad-blocking-behaviors-infographic.html.

McClintock, P. (2019). Box Office: Disney Hits Record $7.67B in 2019 Global Revenue as 'Lion King' Nears $1B. *The Hollywood Reporter.* Retrieved from https://www.hollywoodreporter.com/news/box-office-disney-hits-record-767b-2019-global-ticket-sales-1227497.

Rothenberg, R. (1999). An Advertising Power, But Just What Does Doubleclick Do. *New York Times, 22,* 14.

5

The Attention Economy Is Coming (Fast)

I must warn the reader that this chapter should be read with care, for I have not the skill to make myself clear to those who do not wish to concentrate their attention.

Jean-Jacques Rousseau, The Social Contract, 1762

5.1 Drawing High Attention to Low Attention

5.1.1 Human Capacity

Have you ever walked into a shopping centre to buy a pair of jeans and walked out with two pair of shoes and a new best friend from the cosmetics pop-up counter? That's okay, turns out you are normal. We live in an age of extreme distraction where our capacity to process in a world of unrivalled distraction is limited. So, to efficiently avoid attention overwhelm, our cognitive limits force us to take decision shortcuts. And it seems that the human mind is content with decisions that are simply 'good enough', so it allocates just enough attention to achieve that end. It's called 'satisficing', a term coined by Nobel award economist, Herbert Simon, to communicate the combination of satisfy and suffice. The reality check is that 'satisficing'

K. Nelson-Field, *The Attention Economy and How Media Works*,
https://doi.org/10.1007/978-981-15-1540-8_5

falls far short of the zealous undivided attention that marketers (and philosophical writers like Jean-Jacques Rousseau) idealise and chase.

Consumer buying behaviour is largely habitual and trivial, that we know from decades of consumer behaviour research. When you combine that with a limited human capacity to pay attention, the stark reality is that advertising is incidental in our lives. It's just not as important to people as AdLand had imagined. Another Factfulness moment. That alone is enough to create a crisis of attention, regardless of the ever-increasing demands on the human mind. Marketers are forced to re-think how to create advertising for greater attentiveness. What mechanisms they might need to engage to capture more attention. How to better optimise the media buy for greater attentive reach.

But to be quite frank, how well do we really understand the complex notion of attention?

REMEMBER THIS SIMPLE TRUTH

We are overloaded and take decision shortcuts. This 'satisficing' means that our level of attention to advertising is far short of the undivided version most marketers idealise and chase.

QUICK EXPLAINER

Satisficing and bounded rationality

Herbert Simon (1916–2001) was awarded the Nobel Prize in Economics in 1978 for his pioneering research into the decision-making process within economic organisations. His research ranged across the fields of cognitive psychology, computer science, public administration, economics, management, philosophy of science and sociology.

Simon is most famous for what is known to economists as the theory of 'bounded rationality'; a theory about economic decision-making that Simon famously called 'satisficing', a combination of satisfy and suffice.

The theory suggests the rationality of actual human behaviour is always partial or 'bounded' by human limitations. These limitations come from three contributions: available information (too little or too much), the inherent cognitive capabilities or processing power of the human mind, and the finite amount of time humans have to make a decision. Simon suggests that the combination of these components push decision-making to be done in haste due to the 'need of the hour'. Therefore the human mind, in many different situations, necessarily restricts itself and seeks something that is 'good enough', something that is satisfactory but not always optimal.

This aligns with how consumers buy today and in particular Andrew Ehrenberg's theory of consumer behaviour. Buying is not rational, rather we habitually buy from a small repertoire of brands favouring one over the others in our repertoire (in line with market share). Occasionally we might try new things but we do not, week to week, seek a better taste, more practical packaging, improved ethical sourcing, a higher proportion of Omega-3 fatty acids, regardless of what the ad tells us we should do. We stick to the products we have bought before because it is easy and we are time poor. For goods that we don't buy habitually we might aspire to find something optimal but when we come across an item that meets our level of 'good enough', and we need it to be delivered in time for the weekend, we go for it.

Satisficing is how the real world shapes our behaviour.

5.1.2 Not All Attention is the Same

In the vast array of attention theory literature, we found there was some consensus among scholars of both attention and, more broadly, dual processing. That consensus relates to what is happening to attention during subconscious and conscious states. It seems humans have a default state of subconsciousness where we have a broad and un-specific focus to everything around us. When we are exposed to certain stimuli (or in this context advertising content), our state of consciousness, and our subsequent level of attention, can change depending on the guidance triggers within. There are two types of guidance triggers mentioned in the literature: top-down and bottom-up. Top-down triggers are considered to be personal and goal-oriented (also referred to as endogenous). For example, when we deliberately search for something online or see a personally relevant ad on a digital platform, we pay high and controlled attention. With high and controlled attention, the ad becomes our primary focus and requires us to think on a fully conscious level.

External and stimulus-driven triggers (also referred to as exogenous) are categorised as bottom-up triggers. For example, when an ad delivers unexpectedness, such as high emotion, animation or high sound, we pay low and automatic attention. With low and automatic attention, the ad becomes our incidental focus which commands less demanding semi-conscious processing. Stimulus-driven bottom-up attention is also known to have a sharp and fast rise (and fall), which has implications for advertisers in developing unexpectedness into content.

REMEMBER THIS SIMPLE TRUTH

Humans have a default state of subconsciousness where we have a broad and un-specific focus to everything around us.

Nothing lasts forever, and high attention to advertising is hard to sustain. Like the vacillating creatures that we are, humans tend to switch between attention levels. And the more hours we clock up of divided attention practice, the more fluid our switching becomes. When the information we are actively searching for turns out to be irrelevant we switch back to either low or pre-attentive levels. When an overtly loud ad bears personal relevancy, our attention level turns to high.

We don't just save the special attention switching skill for advertising. Take a stroll to the shops, for example. We tend not to think too hard while we're walking, we just stroll along in a subconscious state until something triggers our attention. This could be either the signals at a railway crossing up ahead (bottom-up trigger) or a friend honking their horn as they drive past (top-down trigger). Once the train has passed and the friend has driven off, the attentional importance diminishes. We return to subconsciousness and think about getting milk and bread.

QUICK EXPLAINER

Defining our measure of attention

At Amplified Intelligence our attention measure is produced by transposing recorded webcam/mobile camera footage (from a view collected via our real-time collection app) to a second-by-second attention score via a custom machine learning model. Our model processes the video footage of a person's face looking at the screen at five times per second, which significantly increases its depth as a measure of attention. The attention data is then matched with product choice, viewability metrics (connected to a reference point via an ad tag) and sound at the individual view level.

We built the gaze model to consider three types of known viewing in line with literature. In particular we consider:

1. Active viewing (high attention): Was the respondent looking directly at the test ad-frame?
2. Passive viewing (low attention): Was the respondent in eye shot, but not directly looking at the test ad-frame?
3. Non-attention: Had the respondent walked away from the TV during the test ad-frame, or looked completely away from the mobile screen?

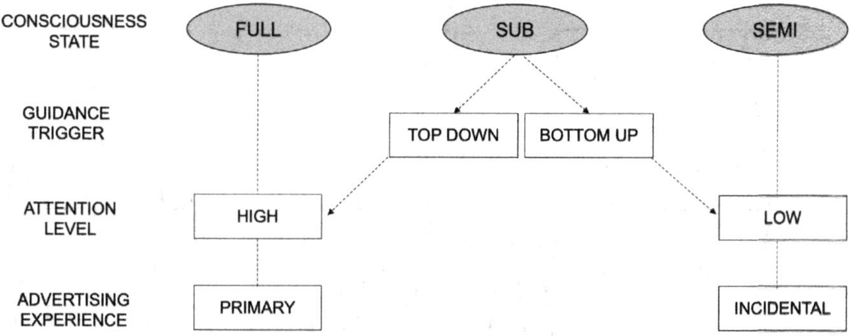

Fig. 5.1 Nelson-Field and Ewens conceptual model of Advertising Attention Processing (WARC, 2019)

There are literally dozens of terms, often used interchangeably, to essentially codify what psychologists call System 1 and System 2 thinking. Figure 5.1 attempts to summarise the expansive literature in a way that shows both the interrelatedness between the terms and the connection to advertising impact. This model attempts to describe the levels and grades that occur within both consciousness and attention. In referring to these levels, Demasio (2000) states '…both consciousness and attention occur in levels and grades, they are not monoliths, and they influence each other in a sort of upward spiral.'

5.1.3 The Value of Divided Attention

Attention research has established that in our cluttered environment we typically process advertising in a low or pre-attentive state. Given this, we wanted to know: in an age where advertising is incidental, can incidental advertising exposure deliver impact?

Over 2018–2019, we had the opportunity to work with Dentsu Aegis Network Global on their ambitious *Attention Economy Initiative*. Their project, backed by a cross-section of TV broadcasters, social media and video-sharing platforms, was designed to challenge how the industry thinks about, measures, plans and trades media, based on a measure of attention. We gathered screen data (viewability/time on screen/sound), eye-gaze tracking and Short Term Advertising Strength (STAS) measures from 17,000 video views in the UK, US and Australia (16 sets of data). This data enabled us to look deeper into the nature of low-attention processing and its relationship to sales.

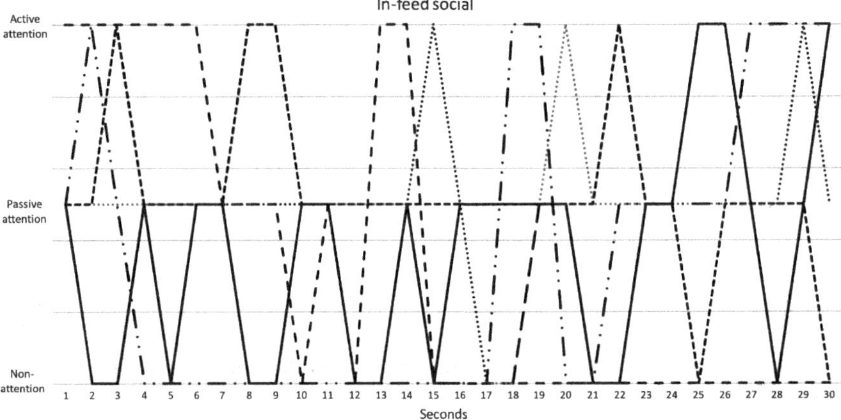

Fig. 5.2 Demonstration of attention switching on in-feed social formats

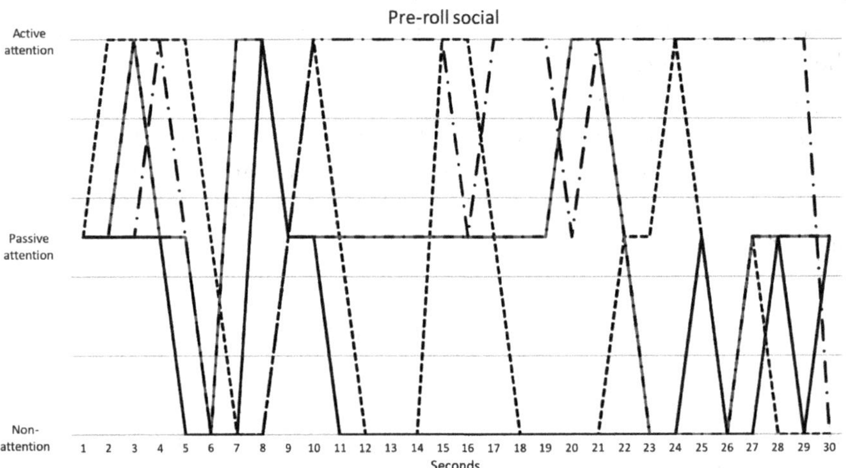

Fig. 5.3 Demonstration of attention switching on pre-roll social formats

It's important to note that the data we collected for this study replicates what is reflected in the greater literature. Firstly, we see that the greater majority of viewing does occur at a low level of attention, irrespective of the platform or device on which the view was consumed. On average 54% (±7) of all attention paid to advertising was low, while only 32% (±8) was high. The remaining proportion being non-attention. In our data we can see that the vast majority of the sample switched between attention levels over the course of ad seconds in view. Figures 5.2 and 5.3 demonstrate the degree of switching between the three types of attention with a small snapshot of our data. It also demonstrates that while the proportion of overall switching is consistent across all platforms, the patterns vary slightly depending on the media type. For example, switching out to avoidance happens earlier on in-feed social that it does pre-roll social.

REMEMBER THIS SIMPLE TRUTH

Viewers switch focus easily. Advertisers need to understand the guidance triggers that snap them out of their normative zombie state.

Next we consider the STAS score by attention level. STAS is a sales proxy calculated from data collected from participants after they choose a test brand from our virtual store (see Quick Explainer). The importance of using brand choice for this type of research is two-fold (greater detail in Chapter 2). Firstly, recall measures are noted to be ineffective for indirect or subconscious exposure given cognitive effort is required to be able to recall and retrieve memory (whereas choice simply calls on increased familiarity without having to be aware of previous exposure to the product message). And secondly, accounting for baseline buying is vital in ensuring that any observed heightened brand choice truly reflects that the ad was noticed, and is not simply a reflection of the brand's market share.

QUICK EXPLAINER

Short Term Advertising Strength as an impact measure

After gathering choice data from a viewer session (as discussed in Chapter 2), we transpose this data to a measure of sales uplift called Short Term Advertising Strength (STAS). STAS is calculated by determining the proportion of category buyers who bought a specific brand having NOT been exposed to brand advertising (control group), and comparing it to the proportion of category buyers who WERE exposed to the same brand advertising (test group). By collecting buying data from a non-exposed control group of participants we can differentiate between real advertising effects and the impact of brand size on buying propensity. This is a key differentiator to the many sales or brand lift studies in the market today.

A STAS score of 100 indicates no advertising impact in that those who were exposed to the advertising were just as likely to purchase as those who were not. A score above 100 indicates that the advertising had a real incremental impact on sales.

Figure 5.4 shows STAS by attention level across all groups. Firstly, this tells us that attention is related to sales, a finding consistent with the 30-plus

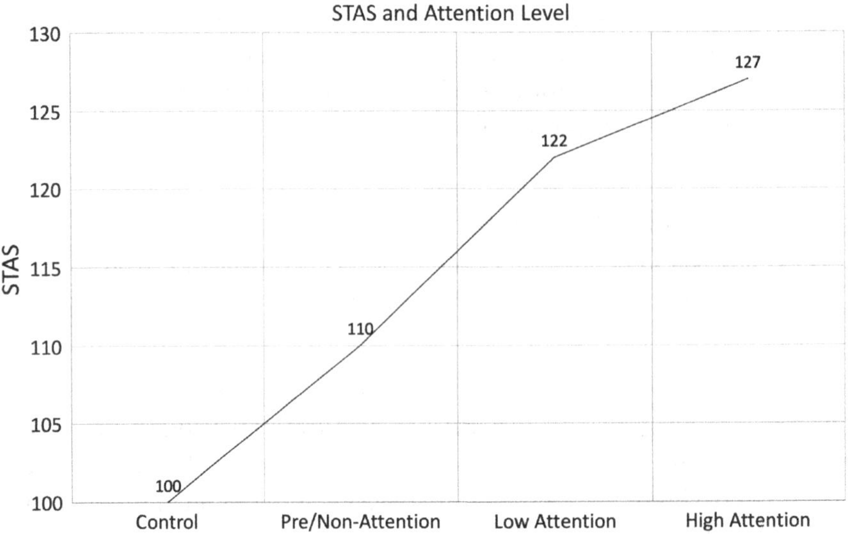

Fig. 5.4 STAS by attention level

studies we have run prior to this collection. But diving deeper tells us more. It tells us that low-attention processing delivers more value than most people give it credit. We found that the greatest uplift in sales impact occurs when a viewer moves from a pre-attentive state (non-attention) to low attention.

Let's be clear here, high attention still drives the greatest impact in absolute terms, but we find that the increase in STAS from low attention is incremental (meaning the biggest jump in STAS happens between no attention and low attention).

These findings echo other studies on low-attention processing and impact in that high-attention processing is rare, that low-attention processing does have an impact and that incidental ad exposure can influence consumer decisions and support the formation of consideration sets. Our work extends previous work on linear TV and gaming into platforms such as Twitter, Facebook, YouTube, Instagram, Youku Tudou, linear TV and BVOD. The nature of our technology and broader methodology in its ability to collect passively and at such scale, is groundbreaking (for the moment). This is a very large single-source collection not restricted by location or sample size or any other biases we speak of in Chapter 2. This work offers modern generalisability and makes a case for cross-platform measurement that truly reflects modal differences and guarantees human presence.

REMEMBER THIS SIMPLE TRUTH

The news is not all bad for advertisers. Low-attention processing punches above its weight in terms of impact.

It is true though, and also important to note, that at the individual platform level, the amount of STAS delivered relative to the different levels of attention does vary. This means that while we can see that low attention does consistently punch above its weight, we find mediating factors can impact how much value low attention (and high attention) returns. This is why we see some platforms are better at fostering attention and delivering sales to advertisers than others. While I do try to remain impartial and not go down the 'who rates as the best platform' discussion, in the following chapters I discuss such mediating factors so that advertisers can do their own math.

5.2 A New Economy Is Dawning

> *People understand the world through stories. Shared stories create brands, shape culture and fuel politics. But a story only has power when it is given attention. The competition for people's attention is called the Attention Economy.*
>
> Joe Marchese, CEO, Attention Capital

5.2.1 A Shifting Paradigm

There is a program on Australian TV, a Network Ten program called *Have you been paying attention?* (2013–) which is a spoof on what, in reality, is taking its toll on our economic and social systems—inattention. Every week the host, Tom Gleisner, quizzes five guests about the previous week's events only to find many fail to recall events correctly. While the program is clearly comedy, the rising cost of in-attention is no laughing matter and it drives the study of attention economics.

Attention economics is an approach to the management of information overload and its consequences on our economic and social systems. It dates back to World War 2 where concern over the distracting effect of noise on radar operators forced inquiry. Today, scholars consider consequences of inattention on learning behaviours, peer relationships, human burnout, organisational productivity, social behaviour, even road fatalities. In the advertising ecosystem the noise may be different to waveform from radar technology, but the level of distraction is still there with an increased number of ads, ad formats and media types. Not to mention second screening, emails, texting, instant messaging, Alto's Odyssey, Candy Crush Soda Saga, Fortnite and everything else in between. Noise is causing significant in-attention to advertising and it's costing marketers billions of dollars each year in wasted resources.

And while the problem of reduced attention to advertising is not going away any time soon, the way traditional impressions are bought and sold makes the issue of waste far worse. Media is sold on opportunity or potential to view and tells us nothing of whether someone has actually seen the ad or not. In this age of significant distraction our current trading currency fails advertisers. It's like going to the store and buying a packet of biscuits not knowing if it will be half empty yet still paying for the full packet. And making matters worse, each media type has their own packet of biscuits which cannot be compared. All of this adds to our declining trust in the system.

Biscuits aside, the simple truth is this: buying on traditional impressions is based on an incomparable, impure and watered down product. Media regulators know this and are trying to work towards improved viewable cross-platform impression standards (more in Chapter 6). But this approach is a long way from perfect and, ultimately, still has the characteristics of a traditional impression. That is, an improved measure of whether the ad had the potential to be viewed, not whether the ad was actually viewed.

REMEMBER THIS SIMPLE TRUTH

Buying on traditional impressions is based on an incomparable, impure and watered down product. Our current trading currency fails advertisers.

Advertisers are rising up and the era of the attention economy is fast approaching; an economy that will see human attention traded as the scarce and valuable commodity it is. The industry has moved from conversations at Cannes to action and applicability. Currencies are starting to form, the nature of measurement is becoming more advanced, capital investment is starting to flow and the study of attention is a growing field. Our own research shows, along with work from credible others, that attention:

a. is linked to real impact (this means real business outcomes like sales, forming of consideration sets, memory)
b. when measured properly, does reflect actual human viewing

c. does inherently reflect the vast modal differences of different platforms (such as pixels in view, levels of clutter etc.)
d. is comparable across platforms.

This makes an economy where media impressions are based on attention, a sensible one.

5.2.2 The Rise of the qCPM

During the American Revolutionary War (1775) the American Congress issued paper money to its colonies as a new independent currency called The Continental. Within five years the currency had dropped in value and was said to be worth only about 1% of face value, causing chaos for the newly independent American people. By 1785 congress issued a new currency, the US dollar. But Americans were spooked from the collapse of The Continental and started trading whatever they had: individual states starting issuing their own bills of credit ignoring the federal government. By late 1792 the Coinage Act was passed to regulate the currency of the United States, and the silver dollar became the only lawful tender. A decimal system followed shortly after.

My point? New economies, and new currencies, take time to establish and they require a unified approach. At the moment the divide between advertisers, agencies and media owners still seems large, but this is not overly surprising given the redefinition of our industry currency will likely result in commercial adversity for some. Nevertheless, attention trading has begun albeit still in its infancy. Unity on the other hand, might take a little longer. It is heartening to see that measures of quality cost per thousand views (qCPM) are on the rise. The qCPM is based on a sensible premise that quality inventory is more valuable because it drives greater impact for the advertiser. Greater impact is worth paying more for, while lower quality inventory is not worth as much.

Understanding the monetary value of an impression relative to platform performance is something we have looked at in our own research over the past couple of years. Our 2018 ROI study used the data from our Australian ThinkTV collection (3 groups, 6500 ad views). It was prompted by the proponents of online platforms (which consistently performed worse on attention and STAS than TV) suggesting that online advertising could deliver better, or at least comparable, ROI to TV because it is less expensive.

This started to form our research question: are the performance differences between platforms accounted for by the cost? Or put another way: how much cheaper do online ads need to be to reflect their underperformance?

Answering this question here doesn't require any reference to what the real CPMs are for the different platforms (although our model did input real CPMs so that we could report STAS uplift for each dollar spent by platform). It required quite simply the application of basic algebra to discern the proportional difference in STAS impact between platforms, indicating what the price difference should be. In short, we found that a Facebook impression needs to be one-third of the price of a TV impression (.34) and YouTube needs to be two-thirds of the price (.61) to generate a comparative ROI to TV (in Australia). We found that these lower performing platforms were way overpriced relative to their return. STAS is not scalable in a real trading sense, but STAS is a quality proxy for attention. The point here being that qCPMs are a good step forward only when q = (real) quality.

REMEMBER THIS SIMPLE TRUTH

Quality CPMs are a good step forward, only when the 'Q' actually means real quality.

Keeping the quality conversation going, some of the earlier qCPMs wrongly optimise for immediate engagement tied to interaction. Riding on the back of the attention movement this 'fracking for attention' (Weigel 2015; Marchese 2019) brought with it a new era of propaganda-based sites (ok, let's call it fake news), poor quality content, clutter, pop-ups and a focus on short-termism. Plus, interaction-based metrics are known to capture a very, very small number of people. Even if the numbers were greater we know this only captures high-attention processing, leaving low-attention impact on the table.

Things are moving quickly, and in 2019 we can see a select number of players building actual 'quality' qCPMs with more robust approaches based on an array of variables, such as duration, viewability, pixels/size, brand safe environment, and optimal frequency. Some of these variables have been empirically linked to attention (and to sales). And some of the applications have now moved from post-campaign analysis to real-time optimisation based on attentive reach. This is one step closer to a true trading market.

We are still in the early stages of currency development. We need a single qCPM to standardise, but there is no unified approach around what the industry wants. Something that's reflected in the varying options we currently see, such as: cost per completed view (CPCV), viewable cost per thousand (vCPM), audible and visible on complete (AVOC), and many more. It's important that we move away from assumed attention units to actual attention units. While we know that things like duration, pixels, coverage/clutter, sound, ad position and content type increase the likelihood of consumer attention, it is still only likelihood. If a human presence is not quantified we are still only working with an improved version of opportunity to see (OTS). Some companies are integrating anti-fraud services, such as, invalid traffic monitoring, while qCPMs such as human, audible and visible on completion (HAVOC) are starting to surface. It's a good start and in the right direction, but not a silver bullet (see Chapter 8, and Dr Augustine Fou in Chapter 9 for more on ad fraud).

The reality check is that none of these are universally accepted (yet) and none of these can spread across all media types, although the industry is working towards this. To quote a founder in this space: 'Changing a 100 billion dollar plus industry is hard…human and viewable has to be the first step…' (Goodhart, Moat Co-founder, 2015).

We ultimately need to work towards a place where an accurate, theoretically grounded, independent 'true north' measurement is created for trading. Where gaze data from real humans (who experience all levels of attention across all boundary conditions) provides continuous learning to the model. That day will come. In the meantime, we need unity before we can move from our own version of The Continental to the attention equivalent of the US Dollar. Once such a currency is established, and a level of trust is restored, we can finally say the paradigm has shifted.

REMEMBER THIS SIMPLE TRUTH

The attention economy is coming where a 'true north' impression will be based on attention, not some made-up concept that bears no resemblance to human presence.

5.2.3 The Wrap up

Most marketers accept that attention is a vital part of advertising success, but many still wrongly believe that fully supercharged eyeballs-on attention will result in cognitive processing and subsequent behavioural outcome. In this age of distraction, the old definition of attention 'taking full possession of the mind' is best left for *The Exorcist* (Warner Bros, 1973). This hypnotic notion is just not reality. But before you call the undertaker for advertising, remember that low attention can be valuable.

Advertisers will need to understand: (a) how to create ads based on the mechanisms known to foster attention, (b) how to buy media that support modal qualities known to foster attention, and (c) how to switch from legacy measurement that only considers high attention, to measures that better reflect the reality of human attention.

Don't panic, the attention economy future looks bright, with less guessing on whether attention is being paid, and far more certainty.

MEANWHILE IN THE REAL WORLD

Putting your money where your mouth is

When Joe Marchese was the President of Ad Revenue for Fox Networks he said the best thing that has happened to the internet is ad blockers. An unusual statement for someone in charge of ad revenue. Marchese thinks (quite publicly) that advertising is fundamentally broken, and the internet broke it. He says that sellers of attention (online properties) don't value human attention; what they value is the potential to make money from the potential of human attention. Every AdTech out there is built for 'tonnage' not quality attention, which in turn is causing consumers' attention to diminish with ad blocking, DVR, ad active avoidance etc. And don't get him started on plummeting CPMs caused by the ad fraud ecosystem in which he says quality content simply cannot survive.

According to Marchese the advertising industry is fuelling its own demise. He warns that either the market fix itself, or there will be no ads. The market will crash.

Marchese has been a loud voice in his tenure at Fox on the value of an attention economy, but his public perspective is not typical of others in similar positions. His solution at Fox? To reduce advertising. He says the answer is 'guaranteed' attention where there are fewer ads that deliver a better experience for the consumer that can command higher CPMs. A win-win. So, he introduced new ad products that respect viewers' time, including giving them an option to watch programming uninterrupted from commercials. Uninterrupted programming is delivered in exchange for their full attention for one long-form ad (that they choose) before programming begins. Others followed suit with similar products including Turner, NBCUniversal, Spotify, Hulu, YouTube and Amazon Prime. These products give the consumer the power to decide how much their own attention is worth.

CPMs should ultimately reflect this, and they do! At Cannes 2019, NBCUniversal presented research findings comparing traditional advertising to 'commercial innovation' ads. 92% of viewers said they appreciate commercial innovation ads more, 76% were less likely to change channels and 85% were more likely to remember the brand. In our own research, which is actual attention via gaze (not stated metrics), we can see that consumers do pay significantly more attention to ads when fewer ads are present. In fact, we found a two-third decrease in the sheer volume of ads, produces around a 20% uplift in both attention and sales. So the concept of pay more (CPM) get more (attention) works.

But who's brave enough to put their money where their mouth is quite like Joe Marchese? In late 2019 Marchese launched a new holding company in the US. The firm hopes to raise between US$400 million and US$500 million to fund the next generation of media and technology companies who properly measure and value human attention. He is literally banking on the next wave of innovation. When it comes to food we've been watching what we put in our mouths for a while, now it's time as consumers to consider what we feed our brains.

Bibliography

Acar, A. (2007). Testing the Effects of Incidental Advertising Exposure in Online Gaming Environment. *Journal of Interactive Advertising, 8*(1), 45–56.

Baddeley, A., Lewis, V., Eldridge, M., & Thomson, N. (1984). Attention and Retrieval from Long-Term Memory. *Journal of Experimental Psychology: General, 113*(4), 518–540.

Burke, M., Hornof, A., Nilsen, E., & Gorman, N. (2005). High-Cost Banner Blindness: Ads Increase Perceived Workload, Hinder Visual Search, and Are Forgotten. *ACM Transactions on Computer-Human Interaction, 12*(4), 423–445.

Craik, F. I. M., Efdtekhari, E., & Binns, M. A. (2018). Effects of Divided Attention at Encoding and Retrieval: Further Data. *Memory & Cognition, 46*(8), 1263–1277.

Craik, F. I. M., Govoni, R., Naveh-Benjamin, M., & Anderson, N. D. (1996). The Effects of Divided Attention on Encoding and Retrieval Processes in Human Memory. *Journal of Experimental Psychology: General, 125*(2), 159–180.

Crupi, A. (2017, May 17). Turner Upfronts Diary: In Pitch to Advertisers, Network Group Says It'll Have Fewer Ads to Sell. *AdAge*. Retrieved from https://adage.com/article/special-report-tv-upfront/upfront-diary/309077.

Damasio, A. R. (2000). *The Feeling of What Happens*. London: Heinemann.

Davenport, T. H., & Beck J. C. (2001). The Attention Economy. *Magazine Ubiquity.* Issue May, Article No. 6ACM, New York.

Folk, C. L., Remington, R. W., & Johnston, J. C. (1992). Involuntary Covert Orienting Is Contingent on Attentional Control Settings. *Journal of Experimental Psychology: Human Perception and Performance, 18*(4), 1030–1044.

Goodhart, J. (2015). *Attention Matters:* Proceedings at the IAB Annual Leadership Meeting, Phoenix.

Greenberg, A. S. (2012). The Role of Visual Attention In Internet Advertising: Eleven Questions and a Score of Answers. *Journal of Advertising Research, 52*(4), 400–404.

Heath, R. (2007). *How Do We Predict Advertising Attention and Engagement* (University of Bath School of Management Working Paper Series 2007.09).

Heath, R. (2009). Emotional Engagement: How Television Builds Big Brands at Low Attention. *Journal of Advertising Research, 49*(1), 62–73.

Heath, R. (2012). *Seducing the Subconscious: The Psychology of Emotional Influence in Advertising.* Somerset: Wiley.

Heath, R., & Hyder, P. (2005). Measuring the Hidden Power of Emotive Advertising. *International Journal of Market Research, 47*(5), 467–486.

Heath, R., Nairn, A., & Bottomley, P. (2009). How Emotive is Creativity: Attention Levels and TV Advertising. *Journal of Advertising Research, 49*(4), 450–463.

Heath, R. G., & Feldwick, P. (2007). *50 Years Using the Wrong Model of TV Advertising.* Proceedings of the 50th Market Research Society Conference, Brighton, March.

Ifeanyi, K. C. (2019, June 19). Must Hear TV? NBCUniversal Uses "Commercial Innovations" to Cut Through the Attention Economy. *Fast Company.* Retrieved from https://www.fastcompany.com/90365757/nbc-universal-uses-commercial-innovations-to-cut-through-the-attention-economy.

Johnson, J. A., & Zatorre, R. J. (2006). Neural Substrates for Dividing and Focusing Attention Between Simultaneous Auditory and Visual Events. *Neuroimage, 31*(4), 1673–1681.

Kim, G., & Lee, J. (2011). The Effect of Search Condition and Advertising Type on Visual Attention to Internet Advertising. *Cyberpsychology Behavior and Social Networking, 14*(5), 323–325.

Lee, J., & Ahn, J.-H. (2012). Attention to Banner Ads and Their Effectiveness: An Eye-Tracking Approach. *International Journal of Electronic Commerce, 17*(1), 119–137.

Marchese, J. (2019, May 29). The Attention Economy Crisis: The Future of Content, Commerce and Culture. *Redef.* Retrieved from https://redef.com/original/the-attention-economy-crisis-the-future-of-content-commerce-and-culture.

Moisala, M., et al. (2015). Brain Activity During Divided and Selective Attention to Auditory and Visual Sentence Comprehension Tasks. *Frontiers in Human Neuroscience, 9,* 1–15.

Orquin, J. L., & Loose, S. M. (2013). Attention and Choice: A Review on Eye Movements in Decision Making. *Acta Psychologica, 144*(1), 190–206.

Pinto, Y., van der Leij, A. R., Sligte, I. G., Lamme, V. A. F., & Scholte, H. S. (2013). Bottom-Up and Top-Down Attention Are Independent. *Journal of Vision, 13*(3), 16.

Recode. (2016). *Fox Advertising Executive Says Digital Media Is Unfairly Screwing Cable—Code/Media 2016* [Video file]. Retrieved from https://www.youtube.com/watch?v=vetRNGEK44I.

Salo, E., Salmela, V., Salmi, J., Numminen, J., & Alho, K. (2017). Brain Activity Associated with Selective Attention, Divided Attention and Distraction. *Brain Research, 1664,* 25–36.

Sauerland, M., Felser, G., & Krajewski, J. (2012). The Effects of Incidental Ad Exposure on Consumption-Enhancing and Consumption Critical Processes. *Psychology & Marketing, 29*(10), 782–790.

Schubert, T., & Szameitat, A. J. (2003). Functional Neuroanatomy of Interference in Overlapping Dual Tasks: An fMRI Study. *Cognitive Brain Research, 17*(3), 733–746.

Shannon, C.E. (1948). A Mathematical Theory of Communication. *Bell System Technical Journal, 27,* 379–423 and 623–656.

Shapiro, S., & Krishnan, H. S. (2001). Memory-Based Measures for Assessing Advertising Effects: A Comparison of Explicit and Implicit Memory Effects. *Journal of Advertising, 30*(3), 1–13.

Shapiro, S., MacInnis, D. J., & Heckler, S. E. (1997). The Effects of Incidental Ad Exposure on the Formation of Consideration Sets. *Journal of Consumer Research, 24*(1), 94–104.

Simon, H. A. (1982). *Models of Bounded Rationality*. Cambridge: MIT Press.

Steinberg, B. (2019, August 5). Jose Marchese's Attention Capital Seeks Media, Tech Firms with True Connections. *Variety*. Retrieved from https://variety.com/2019/biz/news/joe-marchese-attention-capital-tribeca-fox-1203291593/.

Stelzel, C., Schumacher, E. H., Schubert, T., & Mark, D. E. (2006). The Neural Effect of Stimulus-Response Modality Compatibility on Dual-Task Performance: An fMRI Study. *Psychological Research, 70*(6), 514–525.

Theeuwes, J. (2004). Top-Down Search Strategies Cannot Override Attentional Capture. *Psychonomic Bulletin & Review, 11*(1), 65–70.

Wedel, M., Pieters, R., & Liechty, J. (2008). Attention Switching During Scene Perception: How Goals Influence the Time Course of Eye Movements Across Advertisements. *Journal of Experimental Psychology: Applied, 14*(2), 129–138.

Weigel, M. (2015, October 27). *The Fracking of Attention*. Retrieved from https://www.martinweigel.org/blog/2015/10/27/the-fracking-of-attention.

Wojdynski, B. W., & Bang, H. (2016). Distraction Effects of Contextual Advertising on Online News Processing: An Eye-Tracking Study. *Behaviour & Information Technology, 35*(8), 654–664.

6

Buying the Best Impression

Sometimes the questions are complicated and the answers are simple.

Dr. Seuss

If someone says you 'Should've gone to Specsavers', you pretty much know that you've missed seeing something obvious. Made famous by the British Optical Retail Chain Specsavers, the advertising tagline reminds people of the potential pitfalls of bad eyesight, with one ad featuring a vet trying to resuscitate his colleague's fluffy hat after mistaking it for a cat. Not being able to see the signs, makes it hard to realise your end goal. In the age of the 'new impression', where the new normal means paying for an ad that is not 100% in view (or even by a human), advertisers find themselves facing similar pitfalls. The advertising impression at its best is a blend of creativity and technical configuration. In this chapter, I talk about the elements that drive the effectiveness of an advertising impression and impact the end goal—sales.

K. Nelson-Field, *The Attention Economy and How Media Works*,
https://doi.org/10.1007/978-981-15-1540-8_6

6.1 The Relationship Between Being Seen and Ad Impact

6.1.1 The (Long) Path to an Online Viewability Standard

Understanding the relationship between viewability and ad impact is an important part of understanding overall advertising effectiveness. However, in understanding this relationship we first must consider the (long) path to the current online standard. It might feel like a journey to Middle Earth, but stick with me.

Way back in what seems the olden days of media (barely ten years ago), measurement error, non-human traffic, below-the-fold delivery and slow loading were rife. They were modestly reported as impacting up to 50% of served online impressions. This meant that around 50% of online impressions an advertiser paid for were not exposed to a real-life potential customer. And that was effectively money down the drain. In 2011, a concerned US advertising industry came together to discuss a pathway towards greater accountability and to establish a currency standard for online impression counting for advertisers. The bodies involved were the IAB, National Association of Advertisers and 4As, together forming Making Measurement Make Sense (3Ms). There was general agreement that viewability must be at the heart of the metric, based on the sensible premise that if an audience can't see the ad then it couldn't possibly make a difference.

6.1.2 Viewability is a Two-Part Metric

By 2014, online ad viewability standards were set and the US Media Rating Council (MRC) published Version 1.0 (Final) of its Viewable Ad Impression Measurement Guidelines, stating that all MRC-accredited researchers and analytics vendors were to begin counting only viewable ad impressions. For online video, it was determined that at least 50% of the video must be visible for at least 2 seconds to be counted as a chargeable view. While these standards are minimalist by design, they are meant to measure an opportunity to see (OTS) that is comparable to more traditional media impressions like TV. That is, not whether a user, reader or viewer did see the ad in any given environment, but whether they *could* see the ad.

And while most operators have accepted that a standard is appropriate for industry transparency, the push was resisted by online media platforms.

These platforms were counting ads as viewed when they did not appear on the screen and were not actually seen, leaving brand owners less than satisfied. To this day there is considerable debate over both the simplicity of the metric and the standard being set as a minimum threshold. The fact that only a few years after it was set, many platforms are still trading on variations of the standard is testament to stakeholders' concerns.

QUICK EXPLAINER

The most powerful player

Noted by the *Wall Street Journal* as 'The Most Powerful Player in Media You've Never Heard Of', the MRC is a not-for-profit organisation, mandated by the US senate to perform accreditation for rating and research companies like Nielsen, comScore and Arbitron. Media companies paying to be accredited by the MRC, align themselves to the MRC Minimum Standards and open themselves up for auditing (undertaken by Ernst and Young). Each time a measurement firm changes its methodology or releases a new product it requires an audit.

The first of the standards were released in 1964 relating to: (a) ethics and operations, (b) disclosures, and (c) electronic delivery of advertising. Fast forward to 2014 and the MRC released a standard for counting ad impressions whereby a reasonable fraction of the ad content should appear on the user's screen for a sufficiently long period of time. We call it viewability.

6.1.3 But What is Sufficient Ad Viewability?

Bringing national bodies together to agree on a global standard is like herding cats. I applaud the MRC for recognising the need for a standard and reaching agreement on 50% pixels and 2 seconds. But is it enough? Probably not, given the MRC commenced a review of the standard in 2019. Rather than just look at the efficacy of the current standard, I thought it more useful to answer this: what is enough viewability for an advertisement to produce an impact? So, we went on a journey to find out.

We gathered data from natural viewing of online video ads on three major video-supported online social platforms on mobile, in three countries, and across two different years of collection (2017 and 2019). This gave us close to 15,000 ad views. We also had TV data from three countries which we include in the discussion on ad length later. This TV data was not used in all analysis here as there is no variation in pixels on TV—it is always 100%. Pixels being the tiny dots of illumination that make up an on-screen image. If you have 100% pixels, it means that your entire picture is showing on the screen.

For this part of our research, we looked at the sales impacts using Short Term Advertising Strength (STAS) of ads that met the MRC standard of 50% pixels and 2 seconds. From this we could see how variations on that standard might affect the impact returns for advertisers. We wanted to know whether a higher (or lower) pixel count and time threshold returns a similar level of sales as the current standard. Remember, factors such as creative, ad frequency and targeting were controlled for through experimental design (see Chapter 2).

6.1.4 Starting with What is at Stake: Viewing Standards and Chargeable Inventory

The viewability tug of war between advertisers and platform owners comes as no surprise. Advertisers want their advertising to be seen, just like in the 'old' days. However, many online platforms have a hard enough time meeting the 50% pixels and 2 second standard, let alone if the standard increased. This would have an obvious impact on their ability to commercialise advertising. You could argue that it isn't a problem if advertisers aren't being charged for these below standard placements, but there are wider implications. Big media platforms promote themselves for delivering advertising impact quickly through vast, fast reach. From a theoretical perspective, this offers the best opportunity to gain many buyers across the entire customer base quickly (e.g. brands that need large patronage weekly). But if nearly half the impressions don't even make the screen, there is a theoretical mismatch between promise and delivery. The result of this mismatch is that the time to achieve vast reach is not very fast at all.

Table 6.1 represents the reality of the proportion of views that would meet the MRC standard, as well as views that would meet a modified standard. Our data represents two snapshots (2017 and 2019) across multiple countries, offering a fair representation of online viewing and demonstrating why platform owners might resist more stringent standards. The reality is, if the standards were to be increased (which is a possibility given the 2019 MRC review), the advertising model of many online platforms would be affected. If we focus on the pixel part of the viewability standard in Fig. 6.1, we can see what happens to chargeable inventory if the MRC standard was made more stringent based on pixels alone.

Two things are evident here. Firstly, you can see from the 2019 data that there has been an improvement in higher pixel delivery on all counts. A likely result of pressure from advertisers seeking validation of reported

Table 6.1 Proportion of views reaching standard on mobile (varying pixels)

	In-feed social platforms (2017)	In-feed social platforms (2019)	Pre-roll platforms (2017)	Pre-roll platforms (2019)
10% pixels for 2 seconds	89	84	87	95
20% pixels for 2 seconds	83	83	85	95
30% pixels for 2 seconds	70	80	84	95
40% pixels for 2 seconds	63	75	81	95
50% pixels for 2 seconds *(Current standard)*	**56**	**69**	**78**	**95**
60% pixels for 2 seconds	50	61	76	94
70% pixels for 2 seconds	44	51	73	94
80% pixels for 2 seconds	37	41	68	92
90% pixels for 2 seconds	28	30	66	90
100% pixels for 2 seconds	21	19	48	88

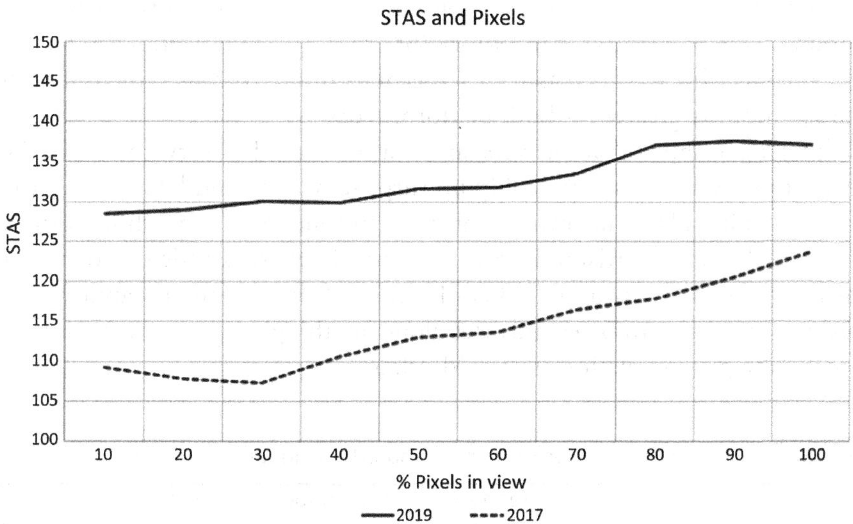

Fig. 6.1 Relationship between STAS and pixels, 2017 and 2019

viewability metrics resulting in both Facebook and YouTube applying for MRC accreditation in 2017. Secondly, it shows that platforms offering in-feed advertising still struggle with attaining higher levels of pixels for their advertisers compared with those offering pre-roll advertising. This is a function of the differences in user experience between the platform types (i.e. ability to scroll, ability to skip and the position of the ad on screen).

In March 2019 the MRC released a call for research in an effort to review the current viewability standards including, but not limited to, consideration of increasing to 100% pixels. Cast your eyes back to the bottom row of Table 6.1 for a moment. In their current structure, in-feed social platforms would be in a world of pain if 100% pixels became the standard. In the MRC call for research document, they discuss the implications to certain media types if the pixel standard were to be increased. It says that mobile newsfeed type platforms with vertical scroll would be hit the hardest as a change to 100% pixel requirement would represent a material reduction in reported viewable impressions. Our data show the same.

Table 6.2 focuses on the time element of the viewability standard. It shows what happens to chargeable inventory if the MRC standard was made more stringent based only on seconds in view.

These tables show that increasing the required seconds in view would be even more detrimental to the platform owners than an increase in pixels. For example, if the standard was increased to 100% pixels from 50% pixels holding the 2-second timeframe constant, the in-feed platforms would lose around 72% of chargeable inventory (pre-roll 7%). However, if the standard for time in view was increased to 10 seconds from 2 seconds, the loss would be significantly greater for both platform types.

This data show that viewers are not viewing for very long on these platforms. While this is probably no surprise, you should be aware that this is why online platform owners continue to tout that (very) short form ads can still deliver advertising impact. Problem is, there is little or no evidence of this from rigorous origins. Let's be clear, if the online viewability standard was increased to 5 seconds (let alone anything longer), many platforms (including pre-roll platforms) would suffer.

Table 6.2 Proportion of views reaching standard on mobile (varying seconds)

	In-feed social platforms (2017)	In-feed social platforms (2019)	Pre-roll platforms (2017)	Pre-roll platforms (2019)
50% pixels for 1 second	66	89	78	97
50% pixels for 2 seconds *(current standard)*	**56**	**69**	**78**	**95**
50% pixels for 5 seconds	30	28	76	79
50% pixels for 10 seconds	16	11	59	43
50% pixels for 15 seconds	8	6	46	37
50% pixels for 20 seconds	3	4	27	23
50% pixels for 25 seconds	2	3	23	16
50% pixels for 30 seconds	1	2	10	15

REMEMBER THIS SIMPLE TRUTH

A move to make the pixel standard higher (than 50%) would be far less damaging for online platform advertising revenue than an increase in view length. This explains why many online platforms are much louder with their arguments to keep the time in view standard low.

QUICK EXPLAINER

Attention and viewability are not the same

What is the difference between viewability and attention? The terms viewability and attention are often used interchangeably (particularly when comparing TV and digital media) and it's just not right. We really do need a clearer distinction between the two.

Viewability is the responsibility of the media owner. It means giving a consumer the opportunity to see an ad on their platform within the standards set by the MRC. Digital ads might load (and be charged for) at 50% pixels while TV ads air at 100% pixels.

The amount of attention paid to any level of served viewability is a completely different construct. The level of attention paid is affected by many factors, of which viewability is just one.

Attention is a consumer output, viewability is a media owner output.

6.1.5 The Results are in on Size

With all the hurrah around making the viewability standard more stringent we became interested in whether it even matters. Does increasing or decreasing either of these variables make a difference to advertising impact?

To consider advertising impact at different levels of viewability, we calculated a STAS score for respondents who were exposed to advertising at each different level of the two components of viewability: pixels and time spent viewing. For example, we calculated a STAS score for 1 second and 10% pixels, 2 seconds and 10% pixels, and then 1 second and 20% pixels, 2 seconds and 20% pixels etc., until we had a STAS score for every decile of pixels and every unit of time for the length of the advertisements. We then plotted these scores for views on each online platform. It should be noted that Figs. 6.1 and 6.2 demonstrate the relationships between STAS and pixels for in-feed social platforms only, given the lack of variation in pixels on platforms showing pre-roll advertising.

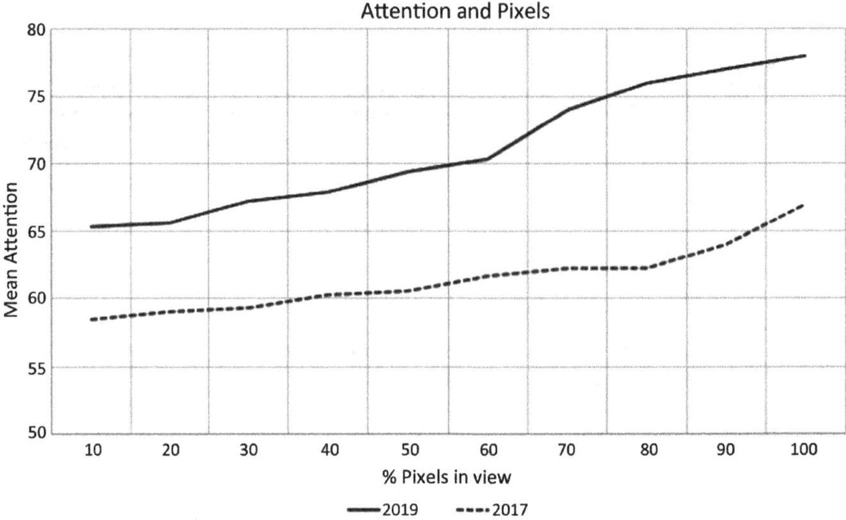

Fig. 6.2 Relationship between attention and pixels, 2017 and 2019

Figure 6.1 shows the relationship between the number of pixels in view and STAS. Our data consistently show the higher the proportion of pixels on screen (any screen), the higher the likelihood it will have a sales impact. This also shows a clear improvement on ROI above the current 50% pixel standard.

With all that said, you might not sell out your entire inventory of widgets simply because one ad is placed on a platform that supports higher pixels. Remember, advertising doesn't move mountains, its impact is small but positive and our STAS data reflect that. While STAS does increase at each pixel decile, the degree of extra sales at each point is typically moderate. STAS is a measure that accounts for market share as a baseline (as discussed in Chapter 2). This means that any increases represent real incremental impact over what would have been achieved ordinarily in market without any impression. That the uplift is small demonstrates the appropriateness of STAS as a proxy to in-market sales.

The point here is not about *how many* extra sales you get for demanding higher pixels, it's that higher pixels does drive extra sales—period.

REMEMBER THIS SIMPLE TRUTH

More pixels on screen typically means more sales. If an ad is not seen, how can it possibly cut through (and be effective)?

When looking at attention and pixels the pattern is similar. More pixels on screen means the ad will likely attract higher levels of attention. Figure 6.2 shows that this relationship was seen consistently across 2017 and 2019 (keeping the groups constant with Fig. 6.1). None of this is hard to believe, if an ad is not seen it can't cut through and be effective.

So when it comes to pixels, it turns out that bigger is better.

The greater the pixels on screen the more likely attention is paid, the more likely a sale will result; with 100% pixels being optimal. This might seem intuitive but you'd be surprised how many people have drunk the Kool-Aid and forgotten what matters most. What matters most is being seen!

6.1.6 The Results are in on Length (Sort of)

The second part of the viewability metric relates to seconds in view. Does the length of time an ad is in view, make a difference to attention and STAS? Well, yes it does, thanks for asking. But STAS and attention are two different variables measured on vastly different scales which complicates their relationship. Attention is measured on a smaller scale, which means that variations will be smaller. STAS is measured on a far greater scale (uncapped) making room for far greater variation. Nevertheless, we determined that the number of seconds in view reaches a point of diminishing returns for both STAS and attention. A point we call the sweet spot. From averaged data, this sweet spot sits at around the 10-second mark, where attention begins to wane and STAS starts to decline.

We were able to test this for attention across different boundary conditions with another data set not previously used in the main viewability analysis (because it doesn't include STAS). The additional data represented the same platforms and same countries but was collected with no creative controls. This means that viewers saw ads the platform naturally served them in their feed; we did not intercept and replace with our test ads. The most interesting point about using the additional data is that while the average attention differed slightly (albeit not by much), the pattern showed a similar drop-off in attention at the 10-second mark.

REMEMBER THIS SIMPLE TRUTH

Where pixels go up, attention (typically) goes up. But after the first 5–10 seconds, as time goes up, attention goes down (and sales follow suit).

You might be thinking that of course the data dips at around 10 seconds because no-one watches old fashioned long-form ads anymore. There may be some truth to this, seconds in view on all media is slowly getting lower each year. In our data, we did see attention to advertising dip at an earlier point for in-feed social than it does for pre-roll; while attention for both dipped earlier than it does for TV.

Interestingly, even though time spent viewing might change year on year (i.e. it *is* going down), the relativity between the platforms seems to remain constant. For example, we see that TV delivers the highest seconds on screen, and in-feed social delivers the lowest regardless of collection year, and regardless of country. Also, there is evidence in the literature that seconds on screen (or time spent viewing in more traditional platforms) is directly related to the environment in which the ad is placed. Therefore, contextual factors will affect the time course of attention.

All of this suggests that 'average time viewing' or 'average seconds in view' is the natural point at which viewer attention diminishes on that specific platform and is a true reflection of the platform experience (such as, content/programming served) and/or modal differences (such as, viewability and usability), rather than any reflection of ad length.

REMEMBER THIS SIMPLE TRUTH

While it would seem that more time on screen is better, optimal time varies depending on the platform. The inherent nature of modal differences means that some platforms support extended attention, some don't. One size does not fit all.

I have one final myth to bust here.

We find no evidence that getting attention early results in a longer view. For example, we cannot see that gaining high average attention in the first couple of seconds, will result in the viewer watching for longer. We can see that average seconds viewed is average seconds viewed regardless of how high or low the initial attention is. Marketers (wrongly) hold on to the notion that early attention must mean sustained ad engagement. It doesn't.

What this also says is that vital information (such as the brand!) should be loud and proud upfront. Every fleeting attention point is precious, without brand presence the opportunity can be wasted (more on this in Chapter 7).

Our verdict on seconds in view: as long as practically possible.

Trying to place a longer ad on a platform that naturally delivers shorter time spent viewing is a waste of time. Sounds obvious when you read it out loud, but most think that their campaigns are different (a bit like most think their ads will go viral, but they don't). No matter how good your creative is, the attention span on that media is the attention span on that media. So being able to achieve high rates of pixels on screen in the first few seconds of an exposure is even more important on platforms where audiences naturally view for less time. The question should be then, which platform will deliver the average viewing time needed for the campaign/creative objectives at hand?

REMEMBER THIS SIMPLE TRUTH

Being able to achieve high proportion of pixels in the first few seconds of the impression is even more important on platforms where time spent viewing advertising is naturally lower.

6.1.7 Could Screen Coverage be a New Game Player?

If coverage and pixels had a fight, who would win? And would clutter be the referee?

As if failed pixel delivery isn't enough, the other enemy lurking on the screen is visual crowding, which is marketing speak for spatial clutter. It can be advertising, editorial, friend posts, comments, other video recommendations, stories, the list goes on and on and on. It is pervasive and distracting and has long been noted as having a negative impact on advertising effectiveness, no matter how effectiveness is measured.

Screen coverage is one way to measure the degree of visual crowding, where screen coverage is the proportion of the screen that the ad covers. It is a proportionate measure and doesn't consider the type of clutter or its specific visual properties (i.e. colour, shape, motion etc.). There *is* evidence that the type of clutter affects the level of distraction, so we plan to incorporate this into our future measure. For now though, we consider the overall scale of clutter.

Before your brain overheats from shifting between pixels and screen coverage, Fig. 6.3 shows the difference between the two. Pixels is the proportion of the *ad* that is on screen, while screen coverage is the proportion of the *screen* that the ad covers. Pixels can be 100%, and screen coverage be less than 100%. But if you have 100% screen coverage then you will always have 100% pixels.

Fig. 6.3 Coverage versus pixels

To be clear, pixels not screen coverage, is currently included in the MRC viewability standard.

Think about it. When you use different platforms the advertising real estate varies considerably. We see this in our own data. When an ad renders 100% pixels on Facebook on a *PC* it only fills 10% of the screen. While for YouTube this number jumps to 30% (from our 2017 data) and around 20% for Twitter. On a *mobile* the real estate is improved in terms of reduced spatial clutter. When an ad hits 100% pixels on Facebook (viewed in vertical) around 30% of the screen is covered, for Twitter around 35% and for YouTube at just under 40%. For comparison, TV on a TV screen is typically 100% screen coverage and 100% pixels. The take home message is that when screen coverage is higher there will be naturally less clutter around the ad and on the screen.

But we were curious.

Given that clutter is noted to have a negative impact on ad effectiveness, and our findings consistently show that ad pixels have an impact on sales and attention, could screen coverage impact effectiveness too? It is, after all, an element of visibility.

In our first series of work (2016/2017), we looked at online platforms mainly on PC and found strong, positive, linear correlations between coverage and attention ($R2=0.87$). Therefore, the greater proportion of the screen an ad covers, the greater the attention paid, and the higher the STAS. Our focus shifted to mobile for subsequent studies, mostly because that was where usage trends were heading. And, as previously mentioned, the advertising real estate on mobile was considerably improved. We found that coverage is more important for larger screens (i.e. platforms viewed on a PC). On larger screens there is greater opportunity for the ad to reach 100% pixels yet only cover a small part of the screen, allowing high levels of spatial clutter. Whereas in most cases on mobile, when an ad reaches 100% pixels by default it takes up a greater amount of the screen, limiting the amount of remaining space and reducing the levels of spatial clutter.

In short, we still see a relationship between coverage and attention (and sales) but device is a mediating factor. For example, 30% coverage on a small screen represents less relative spatial crowding than 30% coverage on a larger screen.

REMEMBER THIS SIMPLE TRUTH

We can see a third possible player in the visibility game. As pixels approach their limit of possibility, screen coverage (% of the screen the ad occupies) becomes more important.

This suggests that screen coverage compounds impact beyond pixels alone. Meaning as pixels approach their limit of possibility (i.e. 100% pixels on a screen which can't physically get any bigger) the importance of coverage comes into play, and this importance is greater on larger screens. In Fig. 6.4 we see that on a large screen an ad may offer greater coverage than a smaller screen, but if it renders at 50% pixels it runs the risk of the brand never appearing.

In terms of which is better, pixels or coverage, the answer is pixels. More ad pixels covering less of the screen is better than fewer ad pixels covering a larger proportion of the screen. More ad pixels literally means a greater opportunity to recognise the brand that is advertising. Whereas more screen coverage (with lower pixels) might still mean the brand is out of sight.

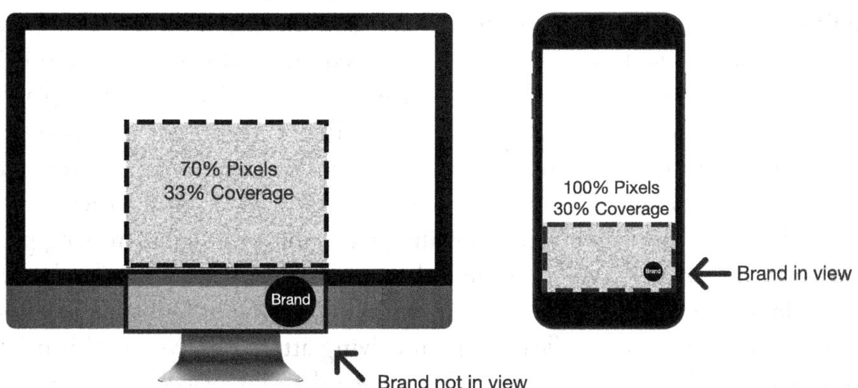

Fig. 6.4 Coverage and pixels relative to spatial clutter

Of course, nirvana is reached when you maximise both, where the optimal placement would be 100% pixels and 100% coverage.

How's your brain going? Overheating yet?

REMEMBER THIS SIMPLE TRUTH

First achieve 100% pixels in view, then maximise coverage.

6.2 Media Context

6.2.1 Is Editorial Context a Magical Missing Piece?

Over the past few chapters we've taken you on a journey to understand the media attributes that contribute to greater levels of attention, as well as what advertisers can expect from the limited processing capacity of consumers. This knowledge goes some way to inform buying and creating the best impression.

You will have also learned that for most of our research we have applied strict experimental controls, holding the creative constant across platforms. This makes the results robust, ensuring they can be truly attributed to the media factor we are testing at the time. But it has also meant that we've never had the opportunity to consider an exhaustive list of media context in our research. And while we can account for a good amount of variation in attention and STAS considering the variables we have, there is still some magic we can't account for.

In the literature, media context is typically split into two categories: editorial context and commercial context. Commercial context includes factors we have covered, such as clutter, ad viewability and placement. Editorial context relates specifically to the environment in which the ad is placed. This could be program/editorial quality (often categorised as expert and non-expert), program induced intensity (high/low emotions), or thematic congruency (where the advertised brand is directly related to the theme).

I referred earlier to *a* magical missing piece, not *the* magical missing piece because no research will ever be able to completely account for human behaviour. With that said, there is merit in the hypothesis that editorial context could play a significant role in driving attention. We see this briefly in our own (albeit limited) data. We can see that ads placed within quality programming generate a 6 percentage point uplift in sales over standard advertising in an ad pod (on the same platform), and up to a 10 percentage point improvement in average attention. This is encouraging, but one set of data with a positive result is not enough for a sweeping generalisation.

You would think determining whether editorial context matters is easy, given researchers (both industry and scholar) have looked at its impact on advertising for decades. But the results are mixed. Literature is filled with contrary conclusions and methodological bias, and is based on testing using recall and purchase intent measures. Some more recent work using remote eye-tracking gives us hope that our hypothesis is correct. In 2019, IAB UK partnered with Lumen and IPSOS MORI to explore how editorial context, and greater contextual factors, impact attention. They considered premium content sites versus task sites on PC. Where premium content is editorially curated by publishers, such as The Guardian and Good Housekeeping, and task sites are practical and task oriented, such as National Rail and Rightmove. They found that advertising on premium content sites resulted in three times the attention of task sites. The IAB did not describe the experimental framework that sits below this study, so we find the results promising but not definitive.

While we cannot conclusively confirm that editorial context makes a difference, the early signs are good. More work needs to be done, but I'll put my money on *yes* for now. I do expect that editorial context plays a role in buying the best impression.

6.2.2 The Wrap up

It remains a mystery to me how marketers can understand the relationship between being seen and ad impact when it comes to ad fraud, but are then happy to accept (and pay for) an ad where most of the ad pixels could sit below the fold. How are these two different? In the first one, the ad is not seen by a human. In the second, the ad is not seen by a human. As much as these types of findings don't help us make friends, especially those who stand to lose the most commercially, the fact remains that there is a relationship between being seen and impact—both attention and sales. The overloaded world we live in makes this even more pertinent, suffice to say I wouldn't be putting my media dollars on a platform where less than 100% in view is considered good enough. And Dr. Seuss is right, the answers are pretty simple.

MEANWHILE IN THE REAL WORLD

Specsavers take their own advice on unobstructed vision

'Media In Focus' (2017) is another instalment in Binet and Field's *Marketing In the Era of Accountability* series. Sometimes referred to as 'the fathers of effectiveness', the duo place great emphasis on maintaining a healthy balance between long-term brand building and short-term sales activations.

In this edition, they profile one company that has ticked all the brand growth boxes—Specsavers.

They say that very few case studies can illustrate the value of a long-term focus quite like this one. Specsavers' commitment to the campaign creative for 'Should've gone to Specsavers', as well as their commitment to a focus on high visibility media including TV (and others such as out-of-home and print) has led to net profit of 129% over the 20 year life of the campaign.

Binet and Field say that they doubt 20 years of short-term activation-based advertising would achieve success of this scale.

Perhaps Specsavers really do value the ability to SEE across all aspects of their business.

Bibliography

Elkington, T. (2019). *Why It Pays to Play by the Rules of Attention*. WARC Exclusive.

Furnham, A., Gunter, B., & Richardson, F. (2002). Effects of Product-Program Congruity and Viewer Involvement on Memory for Televised Advertisements 1. *Journal of Applied Social Psychology, 32*(1), 124–141.

Greenberg, A. S. (2012). The Role of Visual Attention in Internet Advertising: Eleven Questions and a Score of Answers. *Journal of Advertising Research, 52*(4), 400–404.

GroupM. (2017). Gr*oupM Rolls Out Unexpected Viewability Standards*. Retrieved from https://www.groupm.com/news/groupm-rolls-out-expanded-viewability-standards.

Ha, L., & McCann, K. (2008). An Integrated Model of Advertising Clutter in Offline and Online Media. *International Journal of Advertising, 27*(4), 569–592.

Kwon, E. S., King, K. W., Nyilasy, G., & Reid, L. N. (2019). Impact of Media Context on Advertising Memory: A Meta-Analysis of Advertising Effectiveness. *Journal of Advertising Research, 59*(1), 99–128.

Media Rating Council. (2019a). *Media Rating Council*. Retrieved from http://mediaratingcouncil.org/.

Media Rating Council. (2019b). *MRC Issues Draft Version of Cross-Media Audience Measurement Standards for Video; Opens 60-Day Public Comment Period.* Retrieved from http://mediaratingcouncil.org/MRC%20Issues%20Draft%20Version%20of%20Cross-Media%20Audience%20Measurement%20%20Standards%20For%20Video.pdf.

Moorman, M. (2003). *Context Considered: The Relationship Between Media Environments and Advertising Effects.* Amsterdam: Universiteit van Amsterdam [Host].

Pinto, Y., van der Leij, A. R., Sligte, I. G., Lamme, V. A., & Scholte, H. S. (2013). Bottom-Up and Top-Down Attention Are Independent. *Journal of Vision, 13*(3), 16.

Shields, M. (2015, March 5). The Most Power Player in Media You've Never Heard Of. *The Wall Street Journal.* Retrieved from https://blogs.wsj.com/cmo/2015/03/05/the-most-powerful-player-in-media-youve-never-heard-of/.

7

Creating the Best Impression

A man receives only what he is ready to receive, whether physically or intellectually or morally... we hear and apprehend only what we already half know.

Henry David Thoreau, 1851

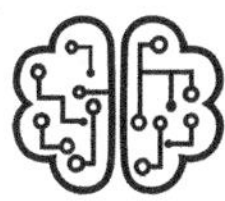

In his 2017 book Robert Heath, an expert on emotion in advertising, said that regardless of having worked in nine different advertising agencies over a period of 23 years, he still believes that chance, serendipity, and stabbing in the dark is involved with great advertising campaigns. While we can safely attest to the fact that we don't know everything, there are a few vital creative characteristics that we find linked to advertising success. A few simple things that make ads stand out and stick. Bottom-up attention grabbers if you like. Welcome to my evidence-based stab in the dark and also to Professor Jared Horvath who explains the power of unexpectedness.

7.1 Attention Grabbers for Advertisers

7.1.1 Attention and Sales are Cousins, not Siblings

I need to make an announcement. To mid-2019, in analysing more than a total of 85,000 test ad views, 52 studies, 3 countries and 9 platforms with

K. Nelson-Field, *The Attention Economy and How Media Works*,
https://doi.org/10.1007/978-981-15-1540-8_7

our system over the past few years, I can see that while there is a relationship between attention and sales, this relationship is not perfectly linear. The notion of attention always directly leading to cognition and then a sale is misguided.

If I said the two variables were perfectly related, you should question my thinking.

Why? Because there are other mediating factors at play. Some of them we can explain with our research, some of them we can't. But what we can tell you is that the direction of the relationship is positive (they move together) meaning more attention does mean more sales (overall). In fact, our regression show that for every 1% unit reduction in eyes *off* screen/ad, the odds of the test brand being chosen increases by a factor of 1.5. When attention increases, the probability of a sale increases. But this is a baseline, and advertisers can improve these odds. This chapter is about the things we know that do move the needle. It's not dark and we're not stabbing.

REMEMBER THIS SIMPLE TRUTH

Attention and sales are cousins, not siblings. They are related, but there are mediating factors that a marketer should know about.

7.1.2 Unexpectedness: Breaking Predictions

By Professor Jared Horvath

Recently, Ben Jones (creative director at Google) dug into the nature of attention by attempting to create the 'Most Skippable Ad' ever. He wanted to see what, exactly, drives people away from digital advertisements. His initial thought was…nothing! If he was to run a 30-second advertisement on YouTube that was simply a black screen—no visuals, no audio, no nothing—then surely everyone would skip past it and he would have a clear baseline upon which to start building a more comprehensive picture of elements required to grab attention.

So, he aired his 30-second black screen advertisement.

To his surprise, almost nobody skipped it. In fact, significantly more people were willing to sit through 30 seconds of a black screen than were willing to sit through the sexier, flashier, more 'attention-grabbing' ads. Oddly, Ben interpreted these incredibly high view-to-completion rates as evidence for the importance of storytelling in advertising (?). What he failed to recognise was that his black screen actually tapped into one of the deepest principles of attention and how to grab it.

We oftentimes speak about the human brain as being a *passive processor*: the world enters our body via the senses, these signals are analysed by the brain, and a relevant response is generated. This picture of the brain, however, is far from accurate. Rather than passively processing the world, the brain is always fighting to stay one step ahead of the world in order to *actively forecast* what is about to occur. This is why many neuroscientists now refer to the brain as an Advanced Prediction Machine.

Believe it or not, you are not actually reading these words. Right now, your brain is about one second into the future simply *predicting* what this sentence says. So long as these words are even remotely close to what your brain thinks they should be, you experience the prediction and not reality. This ability of the brain to make effective predictions is why we're easily able to judge the flight of a baseball, why we're easily able to follow storylines from lengthy books, and why we're easily able to drive home while singing along to our favourite radio songs.

If you ever want to truly and completely grab an individual's attention, then you must *break their prediction.*

When a prediction fails, the brain leaps into the present moment, attention becomes highly focused, and memory networks kick into overdrive. In other words, when a prediction fails, the brain becomes primed to *take in* and *hold onto* new information.

If you've ever miscounted the number of stairs and tumbled forward at the bottom of a staircase, you know this feeling. If you've ever reached for your mug only to knock it over and spill coffee all over your desk, you know this feeling. If you've ever had an animal jump in front of your car while driving, you know this feeling. This process makes perfect sense as inaccurate predictions could prove fatal. As such, when a prediction fails, the brain enters a state that allows for quick and effective prediction updating in order to avoid this failure in the future.

Do you now understand why Ben Jones' black box was such a powerful attention grabber?

When people are surfing YouTube, they have a very specific prediction about what digital ads entail—flashing images, thumping music, a loud announcer, etc. As such, when an ad contains *absolutely nothing* (simply a black screen), this prediction fails and attention is triggered.

This is why view-to-completion rates soared: seeing as viewers were uncertain as to what was occurring, what it meant, or how it would conclude, they were forced to engage and build a new prediction for what YouTube ads entail. Put simply, if you want to grab attention, you must understand your audiences' predictions and break them. In so doing, you will not only trigger attention, but you have a great chance of becoming the baseline upon which a new prediction is built (and all future experiences must refer back to).

But beware: a prediction can only be broken once. Once a new prediction is formed, you cannot break it again using the same material. For instance, now that many viewers have built a new prediction for YouTube ads, a black screen will no longer have the same attention-grabbing power as before.

Keep them uncertain, keep them guessing, and you will keep them paying attention.

But remember, it takes more than attention! Once you've got an audience's attention, you still must teach them in a manner that leads to deep, durable, accurate memories.

REMEMBER THIS SIMPLE TRUTH

If you ever want to truly and completely grab an individual's attention, then you must *break their prediction.* When a prediction fails, the brain becomes primed to *take in* and *hold onto* new information.

7.1.3 Unexpected Emotions

There is an absolute abundance of literature around which creative devices are linked to outcome measures (such as recall, recognition, likability, brand choice), but very few that show creative devices linked to attention. Of the few that do, these 'attention-getting creative devices' include faces, colour, motion, animals, emotion and sound (see Quick Explainer: I can hear you). Although the results are mixed and the measures, at times, questionable, the one single creative device that is consistently linked with attention (and many other outcome measures over the years) is emotion.

The research on emotion spans across a range of marketing efforts, including: video diffusion (viral content), passing down of folklore (i.e. rumours, urban legends, chain letters), email (most reached), word-of-mouth (most shared), and TV viewing (brand favourability). All of which arrives at a common point, that emotions are key in driving further behavioural outcomes. Even more specifically, that *arousal*, an established construct of emotion, underpins this. Arousal is a physiological approach to measuring the strength of an emotional response. It is characterised by 'activation of the autonomic nervous system' or 'heightened sensory awareness'. Arousal occurs during events that, for example, cause laughing or tears, take your breath away, make you sick in the stomach, make you gasp or give you goose pimples.

The idea that arousal is linked to successful advertising (however you define success) is also aligned to the psychology literature that refers to social sharing. In this context, researchers suggest that emotional experiences are shared shortly after they occur, typically in the course of a conversation. It is suggested that the extent of social sharing is directly related to the strength of the emotion felt. What is less agreed upon is the role that positive or negative emotions play (valence). Researchers say that valence plays an important role in advertising success but those in psychology disagree, concluding that in comparison to positive experiences, episodes of negatively valanced high-arousal emotions are equally likely to be shared.

QUICK EXPLAINER

I can hear you

While our early results on sound are promising, our ability to generalise the results is limited. This is largely due to the substantial differences between online platforms in whether advertising is experienced with or without sound, reflecting the default position of the platforms. For example, very few Facebook ads are experienced with sound on, while the larger majority of YouTube ads are. For any cross-platform research project that is collected naturally (i.e. not in a lab), this means it takes time to collect enough sound on and sound off data.

Our early results do suggest a difference in average attention when sound is on versus when sound is off, but without replication this means little. Watch out for more to come on this.

Over the course of the past several years we have done three large-scale and very different studies on emotion and attention metrics. The first two were in 2012 during my post doc years at UniSA and before we had access to scalable and passive gaze-tracking, so recall was the default measure of attention (accepting its limitations to report explicit memory not low-attention processing). The last study was done in 2017 with our own gaze technology (described in Chapter 2).

The first two studies set up a conceptual background for future emotions testing, with our matrix being well cited and applied in content measurement. Table 7.1 shows how our emotions matrix is based on positive/negative (valence) and high/low arousal (emotion intensity) pairs. For example, *hilarity* is the high arousal pair of *amusement* which is low arousal (both levels of humour). Pairs are known to reduce the subjectivity that is often apparent in scaled responses. Two large data sets were used, one of non-commercial video content (n400) and one of branded video content (n400). The ser-generated videos were collected randomly at the time from

Table 7.1 Arousal and valence emotions pairs

Positive		Negative	
High arousal	Low arousal	High arousal	Low arousal
Hilarity	Amusement	Disgust	Discomfort
Inspiration	Calmness	Sadness	Boredom
Astonishment	Surprise	Shock	Irritation
Exhilaration	Happiness	Anger	Frustration

an aggregator site, while the commercial videos were supplied by Unruly (a NewsCorp business). While marketers would be more interested in the outcomes of the commercial data set, having a second set of data with very different boundary conditions adds generalisability to the results.

All videos were double coded, where human coders indicated the emotions they felt in response. We achieved average 89% intercoder agreement suggesting that a wider audience would have a similar reaction to the same videos. From this, we ended up with 1600 data points in our study.

The main take-outs were that videos that evoke high arousal emotions are the most likely to be shared. These findings are both consistent across commercial or non-commercial data and with previous literature. The key contributors to this finding are hilarity, exhilaration and anger. When we look at the combined effect of *arousal* (high, low) and *valence* (positive, negative) on average shares per day, the main effect of arousal is stronger than that of valence. This means that high arousal videos (alone) are shared twice as often as those that draw a *low arousal emotional response* (as compared with only 30% more when valence is present).

REMEMBER THIS SIMPLE TRUTH

Videos that evoke high arousal, positive emotions are shared more than videos that evoke high arousal, negative emotions.

The second part of this study comprises the attention results. Around two weeks after exposure, all coders were asked to recall which videos they remembered seeing. We then matched recall with the individual coder's emotional response. This ensured the emotion experienced by the individual coder was directly related to the video being remembered.

Arousal, as a construct in itself, is likened to high energy and attention. So it's no surprise that overall we find that videos evoking *high arousal* emotions, in both positive and negative form, are the most remembered. In fact, they are remembered around three times more than videos of low arousing content. This is consistent across both sets of data. Again, exhilaration, hilarity and anger are the most successful in memory retention. Although we can see that high arousal negative emotions perform better on recall than they do on sharing. So negative ads are remembered more than they are shared.

The knowledge that high arousal negative videos are remembered is consistent with research on norm violations. Norm violation describes advertising which is considered offensive and outside acceptable behaviour. You could argue content incorporating anger, shock and sadness might be classified as unexpected given the typically positive emotional appeals in ads. But brand risk needs to be considered if norm violations are going to be used.

REMEMBER THIS SIMPLE TRUTH

Videos that elicit high arousal emotions cut through the clutter and are remembered the most.

I've made my stand on recall and intent metrics pretty clear, and it was for this reason alone that I started looking for a better way. The attention and emotions research that follows from here draws from new data where attention is not self-claimed, rather it is collected via our gaze technology. We used 140 coders to classify the 15 test ads in our study base, using the same emotions matrix. The intercoder agreement averaged 92%. Then we collected gaze (and choice) from a much larger sample. The viewing occurred across 3 different viewing platforms (TV, Facebook and YouTube) and 4 different devices (TV screen, PC, mobile and tablet). Our overall sample consisted of 2723 viewer sessions (people) and 20,319 test ad exposures.

We then compared views of high and low, and negative and positive executions with the sales and attention impact that they garnered from the broader sample within our study. Table 7.2 shows the difference between attention and STAS on high and low arousal ads.

We find that, in line with existing literature, ads that are considered high arousal drew more attention and brand choice than low arousal ads. More specifically:

a. Ads which generated a strong emotional reaction (high arousal), irrespective of whether or not the reaction was positive or negative, garnered 16% more attention than ads which elicited weak emotional reactions (low arousal).
b. Ads which generated a strong emotional reaction (high arousal) had a 2.4 times greater sales impact than ads which elicited weak emotional reactions (low arousal).

Table 7.2 Impact by test ad type (attention)

	Low arousal	High arousal
Average attention	50	58
STAS	128	167
Total (%)	78	22

REMEMBER THIS SIMPLE TRUTH

Videos that elicit high arousal emotions get more eyes-on attention.

7.1.4 Not All Cats Trigger Unexpectedness

A really quick, but important note here goes out to creative devices, such as babies, animals, celebrities and sexual appeals—some of the most assumed attention getting devices. Some research will suggest that these creative devices can drive greater behavioural outcomes, and this is a little bit right and a little bit wrong. One of the biggest myths we uncovered in our work, is that it is not so much about the device itself rather the level of emotional arousal that the device, and its context, delivers. For example, dogs simply sitting on a lounge doing nothing versus a dog begging for food due to starvation causes a different emotional reaction. A baby in a crib asleep versus a baby on roller-skates and dancing (remember Evian c.2009) causes a different emotional reaction. So, when a baby or animal video evokes low arousal emotions it has no more impact than any others with different devices.

The exceptions to this rule are political, social or religious messages which do not need to be high arousal to drive behavioural outcomes. For instance, low arousal political/religious/community message videos are shared about twice as often as high arousal videos using these same creative devices. Potentially, this is due to the niche audience segment that finds these videos relevant and appealing. In comparison to general content, which may appeal to a very broad audience, these types of low arousal videos are of interest to a more specific audience. If that video were to hit a mainstream audience, we might expect the level of behavioural outcomes to fall in line with low arousal rates, matching our expectation of a mass audience.

REMEMBER THIS SIMPLE TRUTH

Animals do outperform many other creative devices but only when the video evokes high arousal emotions.

7.1.5 Attention, Memory and the ABC Song

The importance of Professor Horvath's advice cannot be underestimated. Attention is not enough. Once you have an audience's attention, you must still *teach* them in a manner that leads to deep, durable, accurate memories.

But please don't confuse teaching with persuasion. This is about teaching someone how to remember your brand. A very different and vital distinction. It is not teaching them *why* they should know your brand (i.e. brand USP), it is about *how* they might remember the brand at all.

Don't worry about any complicated neuro-marketing that may have been thrown your way, Professor Horvath says long-term memory building is relatively simple. Memory is about associations to context and that these associations need to be rock solid because the brain can easily take you on the wrong path. He says that the more associations, the more rock solid the memory becomes.

This is why attention is not enough on its own. When most of us want to retrieve which letter comes after *N* in the alphabet, we naturally default in our mind to singing out the ABC song we learned as children. We didn't learn about the letter *N* in isolation, we learned about it in the context of 25 other letters that occurred in chronological order. Professor Horvath would bet that you are literally singing the ABC song in your mind right now.

Does this all sound familiar? In Chapter 3, I talked about the importance of building Mental Availability, and here's why. Because attention and memory are not the same thing.

Unexpectedness, or attention grabbers, should always link the brand to an associated cue or set of cues. Cues that bring their brand to the surface of memory on different occasions and, ideally, the buying situation.

This is how we teach the consumer to think of Coke, Vegemite and a thumping De Beers diamond when we are thinking of proposing to our sweetheart at sunrise on an Australian beach. And this why the concept of Mental Availability, and its importance to a brand's long-term survival, is real.

REMEMBER THIS SIMPLE TRUTH

If you understand why we were taught the ABC song in primary school, you know how *Mental Availability* works.

7.1.6 Branding Brings the Family Closer

Logic alone tells us that we shouldn't expect advertising to have an impact on its audience if the brand being promoted is not clear. Yet literature suggests more than half of all advertisements fail to make this advertisement-brand linkage. The content may be attention grabbing, but unless the audience can easily identify the brand being promoted, the material will have no hope of having any impact (let alone increasing buying propensities).

Remember, attention alone is not enough. This is one of those moments where the viewer needs to be taught *how* they might remember the brand. People often assume that the popularity of an advertisement's content aids memory, but it doesn't. Research has showed that highly popular content does not ensure the audience can link it to the brand being promoted.

We wanted to re-test this thinking: to reconsider, with newer data, newer collection processes and newer measures, whether branding quality has an influence on advertising effectiveness. First, we had to code all of our test ads by known branding quality elements. The most notable being, brand frequency, entry timing and prominence. In our analysis, we operationalised these as the following:

Metric 1: Brand prominence—average size of the brand within the ad (%)
Metric 2: Brand duration—total number of seconds with visual brand appearance (%)
Metric 3: Entry timing—first brand appearance in the first 2 seconds (yes/no).

In collecting these metrics, we used object detection software to annotate our test ads for branding elements. Artificial object detection removes the guess work within an ad across all frames. Once annotated, the machine returns answers to any queries or combination of queries the user has.

Figure 7.1 demonstrates our annotation process in action.

Once the test ads were coded we split the sample into two groups by the STAS that each individual ad was able to achieve (based on 14,904 ad views on a TV platform both on TV screen and on mobile). We then considered whether branding quality differed between these high and low performing groups. We found, in line with previous literature, that ads that gain more sales impact (i.e. higher STAS) do all the right things in terms of building good branding quality. Higher performing ads, also:

a. showed the brand at twice the size (100%)
b. showed the brand for almost twice as long (96%)
c. were 25% more likely to display the brand early.

Fig. 7.1 Example brand annotation

> **REMEMBER THIS SIMPLE TRUTH**
>
> Brand size, frequency and entry time all improve ad performance significantly. And it is the combination of the three branding elements that contribute to performance

While these numbers were for our overall sample, when we split the results by device we saw that branding quality makes the biggest impact on a mobile screen. In fact, the improvement in impact of quality branding (combination of all three) on a mobile device is 23% greater than the improvement on a TV screen. Suggesting that where the size of the screen is smaller the greater the importance of prominent, clear and readable branding. Or put another way, the fingerprint of the brand should be relative to the size of the screen, not the size of the ad frame.

> **REMEMBER THIS SIMPLE TRUTH**
>
> The fingerprint of the brand should be relative to the size of the screen, not the size of the ad frame.

But what we did next is even more interesting.

Here are a few truths to set the scene. Remember attention is precious, but it is fleeting, viewers dip in and out of levels of attention across an ad (Chapter 5). And we know attention spikes can be triggered by emotion (and other unexpectedness), but not all attention translates to a sale. We also know that quality branding is related to a sale but it is not related to attention. We don't see visual branding being an attention trigger, but

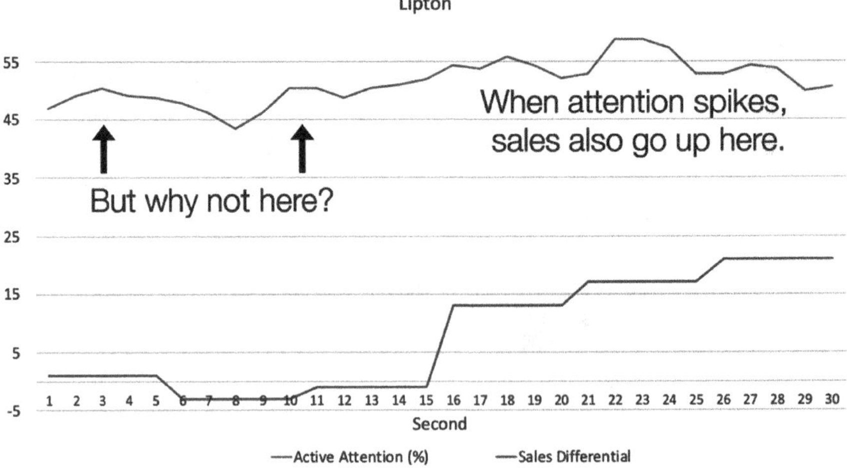

Fig. 7.2 Attention sales differential

neither is it an attention deterrent (something we have observed over many years in this work).

At five frames per second our technology allows us to dig deeper into the exact attention-grabbing moments to understand what else might be happening in the content. Plus, because our data is individual level, we can overlay brand choice for those who did/did not pay any attention. In essence we transposed our aggregated STAS to a second-by-second sales differential against attention.

Our question therefore becomes: what was happening when this sales differential was greatest? Looking at Fig. 7.2 we can see that attention spikes occur right across the ad, but sales remain flat until the last 15 seconds. What is in the last 15 seconds that nudges the sale?

The answer is the brand.

We found this pattern consistently across many of our test ads. Attention without branding still increases the chance of buying, but adding the brand at attention spikes significantly improves the sales opportunity. So mere presence of branding at attention peaks increases the chance of buying (Fig. 7.3).

REMEMBER THIS SIMPLE TRUTH

Attention alone is not enough. Sales are amplified when attention peaks and branding are aligned.

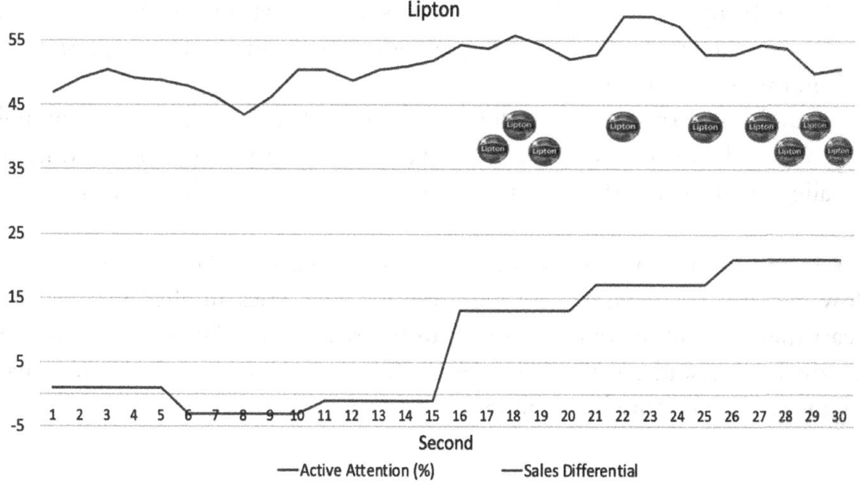

Fig. 7.3 Attention sales differential with branding

7.1.7 The Wrap up

In this book, I and my trusty band of contributors have explained some things that get in the way of the sales/attention relationship. As marketers, some are in your control and others simply are not.

Out of the marketer's control:

- **Attention is fleeting**. Our human capacity is low, we are overloaded and spend little time on decision-making, operating in a default state of zombie (Chapter 5).
- **Advertising is incidental**. Advertising is a small part of our big lives, it is incidental to us and as such we are less inclined to look at it (Chapter 5).
- **Advertising is not a persuasive force and we buy habitually**. So even when we do look at (and process) advertising, the likelihood of influencing an outcome is low (Chapter 3).

In the marketer's control:

- **Top-down triggers**. When something is relevant it improves the chance we will pay some attention (Chapter 5 and this chapter).
- **Bottom-up triggers**. Unexpectedness improves the chance we will pay some attention (Chapter 5 and this chapter).

- **Viewability**. When ad viewability is low, attention will be low and have less chance of influencing an outcome (non-human impressions is another story) (Chapter 6).
- **Brand Quality**. Attention alone, regardless of which level, is not enough. Sales and memory are amplified when attention peaks and branding are aligned and when the brand is prominent and early (this chapter).

Attention in any form is linked to the outcomes a marketer wants, high or low, fleeting or sustained. While attention and sales might be cousins, at least they are still related, and they can improve their relationship with a few media buying and creative rules. With these rules, attention and sales have a chance at being more like siblings.

MEANWHILE IN THE REAL WORLD

Blankety Blanks and the hilarity of prediction

Blankety Blanks was an Australian game show in the 1970s based on the American game show *Match Game*. There was also a UK version called *Lily Savage's Blankety Blank* which ran for 11 years on BBC1. The Australian *Blankety Blanks* was hosted by Graham Kennedy on Network Ten from 1977–1978. It only ran for two seasons, but its legacy lives on in Australia today. Apart from its classic 1970s colourful, yet cringe-worthy displays of sexual innuendo, blue eye-shadow and smoking on stage, *Blankety Blanks* was essentially a comedy program with a game format built around it. The host read a short scenario (often laced with double entendre) which, at some point, contained the word BLANK. The contestants and celebrity panellists then had to fill the BLANK with a word of their own. The BLANKS often lead to scenes of hysteria.

This is a comedic example of what Professor Horvath says in his book, *Stop Talking Start Influencing*, about filling in the blanks. That as humans we try to forecast what is about to occur. He gives an example of how the brain is wired to fill in the blanks when someone is talking to you or when you are reading words on a page:

> Aicvtaion of poragmrs taht fit wtih your prictdeion is the reosan you can raed this sntecne with mimanil eforft – that and yrou'e Pterty Sarmt!

Horvath says that when a prediction fails attention kicks in. Just one of the reasons *Blankety Blanks* was enjoyed by so many and why partners get cross with each other during arguments (although let's be clear, Professor Horvath doesn't confirm the latter).

Bibliography

Bellman, S., Nenycz-Thiel, M., Kennedy, R., Hartnett, N., & Varan, D. (2019). Best Measures of Attention to Creative Tactics in TV Advertising: When Do Attention-Getting Devices Capture or Reduce Attention? *Journal of Advertising Research, 59*(3), 295–311.

Berger, J. (2011). Arousal Increases Social Transmission of Information. *Psychological Science, 22*(7), 891–893.

Berger, J. (2016). *Contagious: Why Things Catch On*. New York: Simon & Schuster.

Berger, J., & Milkman, K. (2010). Social Transmission, Emotion, and the Virality of Online Content. *Wharton Research Paper, 106*, 1–52.

Berger, J., & Milkman, K. (2012). What Makes Online Content Viral. *Journal of Marketing Research, 49*(2), 192–205.

Brown, M. R., Bhadury, R. K., & Pope, N. K. L. (2010). The Impact of Comedic Violence on Viral Advertising Effectiveness. *Journal of Advertising, 39*(1), 49–66.

Cooney Horvath, J. (2019). *Stop Talking, Start Influencing: 12 Insights from Brain Science to Make Your Message Stick*. Chatswood: Exisle Publishing.

Dahl, D., Frankenberger, K., & Mashandra, R. (2003). Does It Pay to Shock? *Journal of Advertising Research, 43*(3), 268–280.

Dobele, A., Lindgreen, A., Beverland, M., Vanhamme, J., & Van Wijk, R. (2007). Why Pass on Viral Messages? Because They Connect Emotionally. *Business Horizons, 50*(4), 291–304.

Dobele, A., Toleman, D., & Beverland, M. (2005). Controlled Infection! Spreading the Brand Message Through Viral Marketing. *Business Horizons, 48*(2), 143–149.

Eckler, P., & Bolls, P. (2011). Spreading the Virus: Emotional Tone of Viral Advertising and Its Effect on Forwarding Intentions and Attitudes. *Journal of Interactive Advertising, 11*(2), 1–11.

Heath, C. (1996). Do People Prefer to Pass Along Good or Bad News? Valence and Relevance of News as Predictors of Transmission Propensity. *Organizational Behavior and Human Decision Processes, 68*(2), 79–94.

Heath, R. (2017). *Seducing the Subconscious: The Psychology of Emotional Influence in Advertising*. Hoboken: Wiley-Blackwell.

Heath, R., & Stipp, H. (2011). The Secret of Television's Success: Emotional Content or Rational Information? After Fifty Years the Debate Continues. *Journal of Advertising Research, 51*(1), 112–123.

Lance, P., & Guy, J. G. (2006). From Subservient Chickens to Brawny Men: A Comparison of Viral Advertising to Television Advertising. *Journal of Interactive Advertising, 6*(2), 4–33.

Nelson-Field, K. (2013). *Viral Marketing: The Science of Sharing*. London: Oxford University Press.

Poels, K., & Dewitte, S. (2006). How to Capture the Heart? Reviewing 20 Years of Emotion Measurement in Advertising. *Journal of Advertising Research, 46*(1), 18–37.

Rimé, B., Finkenauer, C., Luminet, O., Zech, E., & Philippot, P. (1998). Social Sharing of Emotion: New Evidence and New Questions. *European Review of Social Psychology, 9*(1), 145–189.

Romaniuk, J. (2009). The Efficacy of Brand-Execution Tactics in TV Advertising, Brand Placements, and Internet Advertising. *Journal of Advertising Research, 49*(2), 143–150.

Teixeira, T. S., Wedel, M., & Pieters, R. (2010). Moment-to-Moment Optimal Branding in TV Commercials: Preventing Avoidance by Pulsing. *Marketing Science, 29*(5), 783–804.

8

Who Should You Impress (and Where Are They Hiding)?

When we talk of the media, it is easy to forget that they are brands and, just like any other type, carry different values, levels of trust and expectations.

Sheila Byfield, ESOMAR Conference, 2002

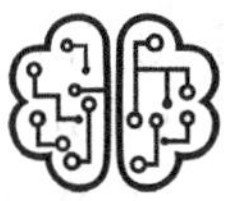

Writing about reach is not as easy as it used to be. On the one hand well-established theory gives us a simple narrative on how to grow a brand. Reach many category buyers when they are in the market to buy and your brand will grow; the best place to find big numbers of these category buyers are in big, not niche, media. But the reality of the 2020 media marketplace is that the value of a reach point across media is not the same. So, are sweeping statements about 'buying big media' even relevant in this landscape? Here's my approach. First I describe who you should impress if you want your brand to grow from a theoretical perspective. That part remains constant. What *is* changing is where and how to find them. Which is why it's useful to outline the practical reality of finding those worthy of impressing, now and for the future.

K. Nelson-Field, *The Attention Economy and How Media Works*,
https://doi.org/10.1007/978-981-15-1540-8_8

8.1 The Theoretical Answer...

...is certainly not 'The Persuadables'. You may have heard of them, they represent the more recent efforts of an advertising obsession with heavy buyers. More on them later, but let's start with how it should be done.

Increasing a brand's penetration rates (sheer number of buyers) will have a significantly greater impact on its market share compared with attempting to increase loyalty—this is not new news. For advertisers, this translates to the need to reach a high concentration of (unique) category buyers across the whole customer base. Based on the NBD-Dirichlet, there are a number of justifications for this recommendation, the most important being that reach-based campaigns are better placed to deliver long-term brand building as shown in Fig. 8.1. Binet and Field's work continues to prove, along with other scholarly work, that advertising that reaches a broad audience is more effective in driving brand growth than advertising that targets a smaller and more 'demographically relevant' audience.

Regardless of the relentless 'hyper-targeting will harm your brand' message from many credible marketing effectiveness scholars around the world, advertisers still obsess over tightly defining the target audience and seeking out only the media that deliver specific audiences. The fact that this will serve to isolate their brand seems to be lost on them, potentially through fear that a broadly targeted campaign will deliver wastage outside of their demographic. Or worse, that they won't see any immediate effect. This thinking is a vicious and downward circle. Those that are most likely to buy immediately are those who are already heavier buyers of the brand. They provide the least opportunity to grow penetration because there are fewer of them than light buyers and their capacity to buy extra is limited.

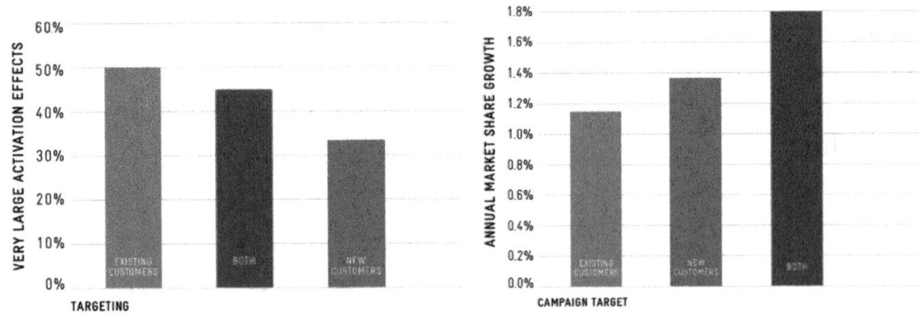

Fig. 8.1 Targeting versus broad reach (Field and Binet, IPA, Thinkbox and Google, 2017)

A recent high-profile case study promoting the targeting of heavy buyers came out of the USA in 2017 by Rubinson Partners, Nielsen Catalina Solutions (NCS) and Viant. Called The Persuadables, this three-brand study actively points out up front that *persuadables* are heavy brand buyers who have been targeted based on the principles of recency. The goal being to find out whether targeting heavy buyers, using recency planning principles, can generate better return on ad spend than targeting lighter buyers. Recency theory is a concept popularised by the late Erwin Ephron, a concept proven as far back as the 1990s. It suggests an ad is most effective when it hits the buyer close to the purchase occasion (see Quick Explainer: Erwin Ephron, Reach Don't Teach).

REMEMBER THIS SIMPLE TRUTH

The biggest uplift in response to advertising comes from simply being exposed at all, rather than being exposed repeatedly.

The authors gathered in-store purchase history from NCS to determine buying segments ranging from non-buyers to heavies (aka The Persuadables). Then, using look-a-like modelling with Viant data, buyer segments were exposed to brand campaigns. The difference in the rate of sales between the exposed group and a non-exposed control group was used to calculate incremental sales dollars.

Let's be clear, their clever use of sales data, look-a-like modelling and technology to target buyer segments during the buying window based on actual brand usage, should be applauded. They have avoided using demographics, which have almost no relationship with actual buyer behaviour, nor relevance to recency. While applauding its use, I will make one small caveat, not all look-a-like modelling is the same and not all data brokers deliver audience accuracy (Neumann et al. 2019).

What is less honourable is their ode to the heavy buyer. Their findings show that heavy buyers who are presented with a brand campaign when they are in the buying window, are significantly more likely (up to 16x) to buy than light buyers hit with the same campaign in their buying window. The authors follow with a recommendation to advertisers to move money from targeting light buyers to heavies. Trouble is, heavy buyers are more likely to respond to brand advertising because they are already heavy buyers of the brand. The chance they will be nudged to buy again in their buying window is pretty high. So, focusing media dollars on heavy buyers is like paying double for a sure thing.

Worse, focusing less on light buyers simply because the advertising was less likely to have an immediate effect, will ensure brand decline.

The only thing light buyers are loyal to is switching, which is why it is a game of numbers. Sometimes advertising will nudge their propensity to buy Brand A, other times it won't and they will choose Brand B. This is why an *always-on* approach has been considered optimal, because light buyers buy at near random rates. At the risk of sounding like a broken record, advertising is not persuasive. Nudging that light buyer takes more than a single campaign exposure, but because of the sheer numbers of light buyers, if you nudge enough them over the year to buy even once more, brand penetration numbers will grow. If you overspend on heavy buyers, nothing will change other than a reduction in profit.

The concept of The Persuadables is at the heart of Binet and Field's short-termism battle. Advertisers continue to be lured by the idea of targeting those who render the greatest opportunity for an immediate effect, rather than those who offer long-term brand growth. Although, at least the study used technology to target actual buyer segments in the buying window, rather than transient data from cookies or other (useless) proxies.

REMEMBER THIS SIMPLE TRUTH

A 16x return on ad spend off a (small) heavy buyer base means less to a brand in the longer term than a much smaller return on ad spend off a (large) light buyer base.

You won't find your buyers hiding in demographics either. To demonstrate the value of category targeting over demographic targeting, a study was done in 2018 by the Marketing Scientist Group. The Persuadables study looked at the difference in value between the types of category buyers (i.e. light, medium, heavy), whereas this one considered the value of category buyers compared to demographic groups. The study focused on uplift in ad effectiveness metrics (i.e. correct branding, likeability etc.) between Gen Z/ millennials compared to Gen X. Overall, it covers an age range of 14–54 years. It then considered the uplift in these same metrics when comparing recent category buyers versus non-buyers for the *same* ads. The study showed there was largely no difference in uplift in ad metrics when comparing across demographic groups, but there was a considerable difference in uplift between category buyers and non-buyers. Again, this demonstrates the value of category targeting over demographic targeting which often bears little or no relationship to actual purchase behaviour.

REMEMBER THIS SIMPLE TRUTH

Demographics bear little or no relationship to actual purchase behaviour.

QUICK EXPLAINER

Erwin Ephron 'Reach don't Teach'

Erwin Ephron was an ad man who happened to understand, and manage to articulate, the implications of media/math relationships. One such relationship was that between advertising frequency and impact. He transformed the industry with the concept of *recency planning* where, he argued, that advertising should reach as many people as possible with the dollars available and close to the purchase occasion. Rather than trying to hit them over the head with repeated frequency until they succumbed to the offer.

Proponents of persuasion theory struggled with Ephron's recency planning, as did media whose commercial model was built on selling repeated exposures. It was in direct contrast to the *effective frequency* concept they had been relying on since the 1960s. Effective frequency alleged that an exact number of exposures has to be seen by a potential consumer before they would be *persuaded* to buy. This concept is still practised today, and the recommended number sits at an average of 3+ frequency.

The theoretical foundation for effective frequency has been proven as flawed from the work of Colin McDonald, Leslie Wood, John Philip Jones and others in the 1990s. In their analyses of single-source data, they showed that the advertising impact from reaching a potential buyer with a campaign was more substantial than an existing audience member seeing the ad a second, third, fourth... time. They not only concluded that a single exposure was sufficient to elicit a purchase, but that the advertising impact on buying propensities was greater amongst those who were exposed at all, than it was amongst those who were exposed more often.

The empirically observed convex advertising response function (shown in Fig. 8.2), shows the greatest uplift in sales propensity resulting from the first exposure, with a further increase, but at a decreasing rate for all following exposures. Two alternative distributions may have been theoretically possible, but have not been observed empirically (the S-shaped response function and a linear response function).

Had effective frequency really been necessary for the most efficient media scheduling approach, then we would have expected an S-shaped response function where the greatest uplift should have occurred at 3 exposures. But this is not observed in empirical advertising effectiveness studies. Nor is a linear shape, where additional exposures drive up buying propensity at an equal rate for each view. The convex shape is closest to reality.

Ephron makes the important point that recency planning never claims that one exposure is enough. That, in the short term, additional exposures are more often wasteful, because the recipient is not likely in the market.

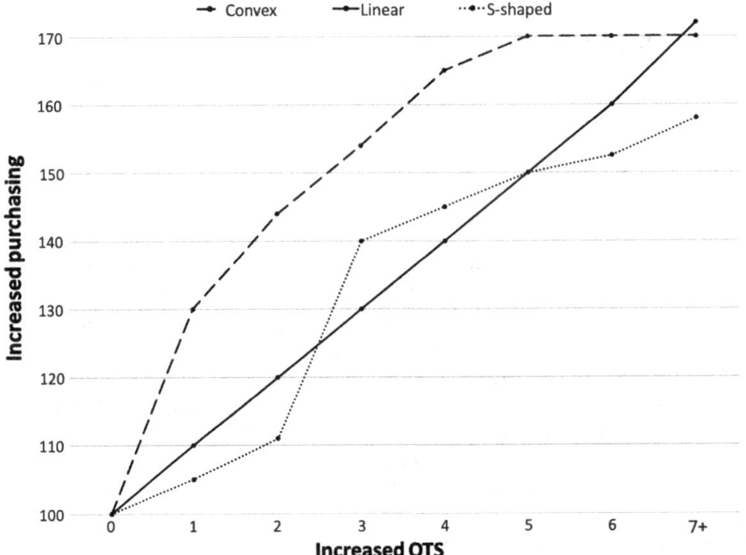

Fig. 8.2 Is once really enough? Measuring the advertising response function (Taylor 2010)

8.1.1 Media Behaving 'Brandly'

We have discussed The Law of Double Jeopardy and The Duplication of Purchase Law in relation to consumer brands. Well these statistical patterns have been found to occur in media too. Big media have larger audiences, who consume (view/read/listen) that media slightly more often or for longer depending on the loyalty metric used. And the audience of big media consume other smaller media less often or for less time, whereas audiences of smaller media consumer larger media more often/longer time.

Stepping back in time to the 1960s, seminal studies of how audiences behave were conducted with the objective of identifying patterns in a person's viewing which could then be generalised and used to describe the nature of viewing behaviour (Goodhardt and Ehrenberg 1969; Goodhardt et al. 1987). They sought to understand the extent to which any two programs were watched by the same people. The main finding showed that just one factor had a major influence on the level of audience duplication—the rating or audience size of each program. They found positive correlations were evident between measures of audience *size* (rating) and *loyalty* (e.g. repeat viewing, viewing hours per channel, appreciation score, etc.). Coined the Duplication of Viewing Law, because of its parallel to consumer brands, the study revealed that viewers of Program B who also watch Program A is aligned to A's rating in the population as a whole. These findings were groundbreaking in their ability to determine a program's level of unique reach.

In the meantime, separate studies on the relationship between reach and viewing frequency found that the two measures varied in a highly systematic way. The relationship was found to follow the well known Double Jeopardy pattern where smaller channels were found to have fewer viewers who watched them less. Both laws were later found to hold in TV channel viewing, print viewership and radio listening. By 2005, the first work on cross-media patterns surfaced to consider how loyal consumers were to any one media type over another. Specifically, how audiences interacted with media across television, radio, newspaper and magazine. The patterns held.

A generalisation was now well and truly established: media do behave like brands. The viewing patterns of media audiences behave just like the customer bases of consumer brands.

By 2013 a study by the Ehrenberg-Bass Institute (using 2007–2010 data) considered cross-website visiting behaviour in UK and Australia. Websites included Yahoo!, AOL, MySpace, MSN-WL, Virgin Media and general sites representing the internet as a category (although these are not defined). Again, the Duplication of Viewing pattern was evident in both sets of data. But, the rise of the super socials feels like it has changed everything—dramatically! Using our Australian 2018 data (1520 people) we wanted to understand whether these patterns hold in the Facebook/YouTube/Twitter-verse some ten years on. And they do. We found that Facebook, the largest reaching media within its direct ecosystem, shares its audience the least with its competitors (see Table 8.1).

Table 8.1 Media size and loyalty (Double Jeopardy within online ecosystem)

Online social platforms ($R^2 = 0.95$)	Market share (online users)	Penetration (online users)	No. of platforms used (loyalty)
Facebook	23	90	4.1
YouTube	19	74	4.5
Instagram	14	55	5.1
Snapchat	9	35	5.4
WhatsApp	8	30	5.4
Pinterest	7	26	5.5
Twitter	6	22	5.9
LinkedIn	6	22	5.8
Google+	5	22	5.4
Buzzfeed	3	11	6.6
Reddit	3	10	6.2
Total/Average	100		5.4

What we really wanted to know is whether the patterns hold across the top competing platforms in the broader landscape. A consideration of those who fight directly for each other's ad dollars. And, yes, they do hold.

Of Facebook users 75% also watch TV, and 87% of TV viewers also use Facebook. Snapchat shares its audience most with its competitors, which is as expected and in line with its market share. What this says is that overall the very large majority of any competing media audience (92%) can also be accessible with a Facebook campaign.

REMEMBER THIS SIMPLE TRUTH

All media types display Double Jeopardy: larger media have more people who view/read/listen more often. All media types display Duplication of Viewing: larger media share their audience less with smaller media.

So, you get the gist. These mathematical patterns hold within and across the very large majority of media, regardless of this crazy media landscape we find ourselves in. The point is, that there are some benefits of being the largest penetration media brand. The most bleedingly obvious is that bigger media give advertisers potential access to greater numbers of viewers who also view slightly more often/for a longer period and, consequently, have the greatest access to category buyers. Larger media also deliver the largest proportion of *unique reach*. This is why the Duplication of Viewing Law is so handy. We can use it to understand the extent to which any two media type/channels/programs are watched by the same people in the same period.

So, when we say that 75% of Facebook users also watch TV, this means that around one-quarter of Facebook reach is unique and cannot be reached by a TV campaign. And around 13% of TV viewers are unique and cannot be reached by Facebook. This is valuable information in the absence of access to single-source media mix planners, and particularly helpful when planning a multi-platform buy. Any addition of a media type to the media mix will, to an extent, simply add exposure frequency to the campaign, rather than building additional unique reach.

It is upon this knowledge that marketing effectiveness scholars advise advertisers to buy the largest media available for their budget (to maximise reach).

But ad fraud changes everything.

8.2 The Practical Reality

Let me give you one truth. If you added up the ROI metrics that are espoused by many, many publishers, many, many data providers, the U.S. GDP would double every six months. There's so much BS in the marketplace.

Steve Hasker, Chief Operating Officer, Nielsen

8.2.1 Big Media May Not Be Big

I promised to describe who you should impress from a theoretical perspective, and I have.

A brand needs to focus on reaching as many category buyers as possible, rather than hyper-targeting any single (reportedly relevant) demographic group, or buying segment.

The statistical laws that underpin a media audience should help an advertiser understand where to find these category buyers, but in 2020 all bets are off. Sweeping statements about *buying big media* are not relevant in this landscape. While we see that the Duplication of Viewing and Double Jeopardy patterns are still evident in our data, our sample is experimentally controlled to expose real humans to real ad impressions in real viewing environments, 100% of the time. This is not the reality of the online video market.

Today there is a flourishing business in click farms, ad stacking, duplicate accounts, fake accounts, fake views, fake subscribers, fake shares, fake followers, fake influencers, fake ads, cookie stuffing and fake things we haven't heard of yet. And this brings us back to the half empty packet of biscuits. This means that buying reach from big online media, but not knowing how many impressions are real, might not actually deliver any unique viewers at all—depends on the luck of the distribution that lies beneath (which a marketer will never know).

REMEMBER THIS SIMPLE TRUTH

Buying reach from big online media, but not knowing how many impressions are real, might not actually deliver any unique viewers at all.

In terms of fake and duplicate accounts even Facebook struggles to report the scale of the problem, stating in a securities filing in October 2018 that, 'Duplicate and false accounts are very difficult to measure at our scale,' and the actual numbers, '...may vary significantly from our estimates'. When

New York Times reporter Jack Nicas asked Alex Schultz, Facebook's Vice President of Analytics how advertisers felt about paying to show ads to fake accounts, Mr. Schultz said, 'What advertisers need to feel comfortable about are the actual results generated by our ad campaigns'.

An interesting take from Facebook, but not knowing what reach you are getting for your money is like walking into a car dealership with a blank cheque and a cheesy salesmen saying, 'Trust me little lady all you need to know is that your dream car drives, you don't need to know what's under the hood'. This feels like what many of the major platforms say when questioned about their inner workings. In Australia in 2018, when the Government-mandated Australian Competition and Consumer Commission (ACCC) asked for a response from the digital platforms to complaints raised against them in the Digital Platforms Inquiry (see Chapter 1), the Chairman of the ACCC said the response from the 'dominant digital platforms' might be best described as a 'trust us' reply.

On fraud more specifically, the World Federation of Advertisers (WFA) in their 2017 ad fraud report, talk about the industry as having deep structural issues of which they suggest will likely get worse with a 22% year-on-year growth for fraudulent bot traffic. They suggest that bots inflate monetised audience by 5% to 50% and report the scale of the problem to be quite substantial:

- 88% of digital ad clicks deemed fraudulent
- bot traffic is up to 61.5% of all website traffic
- 40% of mobile ad clicks are essentially worthless
- more than 18% of impressions come from bots.

A team from the University of Twente in the Netherlands wrote a paper in 2018 describing the business model of a botnet (fraud network), suggesting that botnets, in particular click fraud, are a hugely profitable undertaking for those who are successful. The team predicts profit per month for a syndicate can be in excess of US$20 million. In 2019, Dr. Augustine Fou, a cybersecurity and ad fraud researcher, wrote about research cases where all of the sessions from a particular website or platform were turned off, yet there was no change to the goal events recorded (i.e. impression completions). Meaning, that none of the goal events were driven by visitors from that source, they were bots. He suggests that brands who are treating digital as a reach in frequency medium, are being duped in that most ad impressions across display ad and video, and mobile ad impressions are made up.

It's important to note that ad fraud is an internet thing, not a platform thing, so TV is not immune. As the future of TV moves to over-the-top (OTT) services, where video content is served via the internet rather than the traditional closed television system, ad fraud will become more apparent. OTT ad fraud is reported to sit at about 19% globally at the moment and is on the rise (Pixalate, an MRC accredited OTT invalid traffic detection company, 2018).

> **REMEMBER THIS SIMPLE TRUTH**
>
> Ad fraud is not a Facebook, Google, Twitter thing—it is an internet thing and TV is not immune as it moves towards OTT.

Despite all of this, of the reach that does hit a real human, the value of those reach points is diminished by the nature of the platform's ability to deliver appropriate viewability (as per Chapter 5). So, when we say that one-quarter of Facebook reach is unique to that of TV, which on the surface seems a decent advantage, the likelihood of that 25% being: (a) seen by a human consumer, and (b) truly unduplicated, and (c) of a high viewable delivery, is extremely low. So, it would seem that any apparent advantages of gaining unique reach from the bigger online platforms are seriously watered down by the reality of what lies beneath.

> **REMEMBER THIS SIMPLE TRUTH**
>
> Sweeping statements about *buying big media* are out of touch in this landscape. When a platform is twice as big, but a reach point delivers half the pixels to half the humans, half of which are duplicate accounts, any value in being *big* is cancelled out.

8.2.2 Coming Full Circle

Given its relationship to penetration, reach is vital. And reaching many category buyers through purchase-based targeting, where purchase data is used to build look-a-like consumer segments for targeting close to the purchase occasion, might be the holy grail. But when the platforms that have the greatest capability to roll out look-a-like targeting are the greatest culprits of poor and/or fraudulent ad delivery, it poses a BIG problem for finding where category buyers are hiding.

Until a silver bullet, or maybe an anti-bacterial wipe, is applied to our industry to clean up online inventory, a new parameter should be applied in the media buy—*reach quality*. Only after reach quality per thousand impressions is assessed should traditional parameters, such as unique reach, overall cost and cost to target market speed of delivery (accumulating reach), be considered.

In terms of quantifying reach quality, we look to our own research on reach quality, the WFA ad fraud guidelines, Dr Fou and some in-the-trenches platinum-level advertisers, for a baseline list. It's a list that covers media factors only; things about the delivery of the reach point that make the impression valuable. It does not include considerations of viewer behaviour (such as, rate of engagement, scroll speed, conversions, time spent viewing) or other campaign factors (such as, relevance, targeting ability, creative restrictions, ad placement or brand safety). You may have noted that many of these were discussed in the qCPM section of Chapter 5. For quality reach, common-sense parameters might include:

- % pixels on screen
- # seconds in view
- % screen coverage
- % ad clutter
- % sound on
- % likely human impressions (fraud estimation counts)
- % account/viewer duplication.

The WFA suggests that advertisers demand full transparency from the media owner on likelihood of human impression and account/viewer duplication, not simply accept what is available publicly. Additionally, Dr Fou calls out to advertisers to run their own #turnoffadtech experiments to ascertain the level of traffic that is fraudulent. That's right, he's suggesting that advertisers should cut budget for a period of time to see how goal events change. If there is no change, that is telling. Also build a white list of accepted sites (those who supply transparency, tick the brand safety requirement and are verified by IAS, DV, MOAT, etc.), and stick to these.

QUICK EXPLAINER

World Federation of Advertisers (WFA)

WFA is a global not-for-profit organisation representing the common interests of client-side marketers (not agencies, media owners or vendors). Its global membership represents roughly 90% of all the global marketing communications spend, almost US$900 billion annually.

Founded in Italy in 1953 the WFA is based in Brussels, Belgium and has offices in London and Singapore.

WFA helps its members to improve the effectiveness and efficiency of their marketing communications through benchmarking and the sharing of knowledge, experiences and insights. It provides a unique global network of marketers who help each other navigate the fast-changing marketing landscape.

It also champions and defends marketers interests, helps set standards for responsible marketing communications worldwide and encourages leadership initiatives, which go beyond compliance with existing industry standards.

8.2.3 The Wrap up

Quality reach is out there, it's just harder to find than it used to be and it is not simply going to be handed to you by the biggest media. But quality reach is worth paying for and it can pay dividends both in terms of ROI and brand growth. As the industry evolves and AdTech is called to account, quality CPMs will become more advanced. And the day when q = (real) quality, the ground advertisers have lost will slowly be reclaimed.

MEANWHILE IN THE REAL WORLD

When machines decide the bubbles, Peppa Pig pays the price

Online behavioural advertising, or more specifically the targeting technology that uses past behaviour to infer targeting options, operates in a filter bubble. It is based on a machine learning algorithm that may be accurate at one point in time, but over time can become separated from its source point reality. And it can go hilariously wrong.

In 2017 IAG, Australia's largest general insurer, underwent an attribution project which included a series of media experiments to understand advertising ROI for each marketing channel. One of the experiments revolved around understanding the causal impact of retargeting. Matthew Daniell, IAG Effectiveness Lead, told audiences at a Mumbrella 360 event in Sydney

(2019) that what they found (by accident) was weird, hilarious and scary all at the same time. According to the DSP, the most over-indexing audience trait compared with IAG buying data was…nappies. Not 'In-Market for Car Insurance', not 'In-Market for Home Insurance', or any car/home related targeting, but nappies. Yet according to the same buying data, 60% of their customers are not parents.

Matthew went on to explain that while car insurance signals might start out as 'searching for a car', the pool of signals collected on relevant sites is small. But brands need reach to grow, so to increase audience numbers to acceptable levels of reach, a look-a-like algorithm takes characteristics from what it perceives as similar groups of people. Problem is, sometimes the larger audience display unrelated, but dominant, characteristics (like nappies) and this is when things can go bad. This is what happened for IAG and their ads ended up as pre-rolls on Peppa Pig, Paw Patrol and Toy Unboxing. For IAG, every ad that is served against a kids' video is wasted money.

Most data brokers have secret black-box systems, so these mistakes are hard to uncover, and even more difficult to rectify. Matthew questions, at what point does behavioural targeting go from an insight to a useless data point. How often do we have faith that these audiences are real? And how often are targeting options not checked? IAG spend a great deal of time creating strict placement and topic blacklists, but it is a never-ending task and not always adhered to. He says there always seems to be somewhere in the supply chain that can get around these lists.

Bob Hoffman, Ad Contrarian, says: Technology without wisdom is just an elevator without buttons.

Matthew Daniell, IAG, says: I would rather know which floor the elevator will stop.

I say: *When you have to black list Peppa Pig, something is clearly wrong.*

Bibliography

Agostini, J. M. (1961). How to Estimate Unduplicated Audiences. *Journal of Advertising Research, 1*(3), 11–14.

Agostini, J. M. (1962). Analysis of Magazine Accumulative Audiences. *Journal of Advertising Research, 2*(1), 24–27.

Barwise, P., & Ehrenberg, A. (1988). *Television and Its Audience*. London: Sage.

Beal, V. (2003). *Patterns in Television Viewing Behaviour: What's Changed Since the 1980's?* (p. 154). Marketing Science Centre, University of South Australia, Master of Business (Research), Adelaide.

Binet, L., & Field, P. (2017). *Media in Focus: Marketing Effectiveness in the Digital Era*. Institute of Practitioners in Advertising.

Byfield, S. (2002, June). Media *Under Threat? Who Will Survive*. European Society for Opinion and Marketing Research.

Cannon, H. M., & Riordan, E. A. (1994). Effective Reach and Frequency: Does It Really Make Sense? *Journal of Advertising Research, 34*(2), 19–28.

Corkindale, D. R., Romaniuk, J., & Driesener, C. (2013). *How the Duplication of Viewing Law Applies to Website Visiting and Some Implications* (Doctoral dissertation). ANZMAC-Australian and New Zealand Marketing Academy.

Ehrenberg, A. S. C. (1981). Who Watches Repeats? *Broadcast, 1139*(12).

Ehrenberg, A. S. C., Uncles, M. D., & Goodhardt, G. G. (2004). Understanding Brand Performance Measures: Using Dirichlet Benchmarks. *Journal of Business Research, 57*(12), 1307–1325.

Ephron, E. (1995). More Weeks, Less Weight: The Shelf-Space Model of Advertising. *Journal of Advertising Research, 35*(3), 18–23.

Ephron, E. (1998). Point of View: Optimizers and Media Planning. *Journal of Advertising Research, 38*(4), 47–56.

Ephron, E., & Heath, M. (2001). Once May Not Be Enough, But It's the Best We Can Do. *Admap, 36*(10), 44–46.

Fou, A. (2019, July 16). The #turnoffadtech Movement Is Gaining Momentum [LinkedIn post]. *LinkedIn*. Retrieved from https://www.linkedin.com/pulse/turnoffadtech-movement-gaining-momentum-ad-fraud-historian/?trk=related_artice_The%20%23TurnOffAdtech%20Movement%20is%20Gaining%20Momentum_article-card_title.

Goodhardt, G. J. (1966, December 31). Constant in Duplicated Television Viewing. *Nature, 212*, 1616.

Goodhardt, G. J., & Ehrenberg, A. S. C. (1969). Duplication of Television Viewing Between and Within Channels. *Journal of Marketing Research, 6*, 169–178.

Goodhardt, G. J., Ehrenberg, A. S. C., & Collins, M. A. (1987). *The Television Audience—Patterns of Viewing: An Update*. Hants, UK: Gower Publishing.

Hammer, P. (2017, February 22). *The ABC of XYZ* [LinkedIn post]. Retrieved from https://www.linkedin.com/pulse/age-just-another-number-peter-hammer.

Kotila, M., Rumin, R. C., & Dhar, S. (2016). Compendium of Ad Fraud Knowledge for Media Investors. *WFA Global Transparency Group*.

Lees, G. (2005). *Is There a Double Jeopardy Effect with Radio Listening Behaviour* (ANZMAC Paper).

McDonald, C. (1992). *How Advertising Works: A Review of Current Thinking*. Henley-on-Thames, UK: Advertising Association in conjunction with NTC Publications Ltd.

McDonald, C. (2000). *Television Audience Measurement*. WARC Best Practice.

McDowell, W. S., & Dick, S. J. (2005). Revealing a Double Jeopardy Effect in Radio Station Audience Behaviour. *Journal of Media Economics, 18*(4), 271–284.

Nelson-Field, K., & Riebe, E. (2011). The Impact of Media Fragmentation on Audience Targeting: An Empirical Generalisation Approach. *Journal of Marketing Communications, 17*(1), 51–67.

Neumann, N., Tucker, C., & Whitfield, T. (2019, October 2). Frontiers: How Effective Is Third-Party Consumer Profiling and Audience Delivery? Evidence from Field Studies. *Marketing Science*, 1–9. https://doi.org/10.1287/mksc.2019.1188.

Nicas, J. (2019). Does Facebook Really Know How Many Fake Accounts It Has? *New York Times*. Retrieved from https://www.nytimes.com/2019/01/30/technology/facebook-fake-accounts.html.

Pixalate. (2018, November 19). OTT Ad Fraud Is a Growing Threat, and You Need to Know More About It. *Pixalate*. Retrieved from http://blog.pixalate.com/what-is-ott-connected-tv-ad-fraud.

Putman, C. G. J., & Nieuwenhuis, L. J. (2018, March). Business Model of a Botnet. In *26th Euromicro International Conference on Parallel, Distributed and Network-Based Processing* (PDP) (pp. 441–445). IEEE.

Redden, P. (2017). *What Matters in Media: An Investigation of Media Decision Makers' Perceptions of Value* (Masters thesis). University of South Australia, Adelaide.

Redford, N. (2005). *Regularities in Media Consumption* (Masters thesis). University of South Australia, Adelaide.

Rogers, B. (2019, January 18). Will It Take an AdTech Crash to End Digital Ad Fraud? *Forbes*. Retrieved from https://www.forbes.com/sites/brucerogers/2019/01/18/will-it-take-an-adtech-crash-to-end-digital-ad-fraud/#5925b55d1368.

Rubinson Partners, Inc. (2017). Revealing the Return on Recency. *NCSolutions*. Retrieved from https://www.ncsolutions.com/case-studies/revealing-return-recency/#more-2745.

Sharp, B. (2010). *How Brands Grow*. Melbourne: Oxford University Press.

Taylor, J. (2010). *Is Once Really Enough? Measuring the Advertising Response Function* (Unpublished PhD thesis). University of South Australia, Adelaide.

Taylor, J., Kennedy, R., McDonald, C., Larguinat, L., El Ouarzazi, Y., & Haddad, N. (2013). Is the Multi-platform Whole More Powerful Than Its Separate Parts? Measuring the Sales Effects of Cross-Media Advertising. *Journal of Advertising Research, 53*(2), 200–211.

Taylor, J., Kennedy, R., & Sharp, B. (2009). Making Generalizations About Advertising's Convex Sales Response Function: Is Once Really Enough? *Journal of Advertising Research, 49*(2), 198–200.

Vakratsas, D., & Ambler, T. (1999). How Advertising Works: What Do We Really Know? *Journal of Marketing, 63*(1), 26–43.

9

The Magic 8 Ball

People can foresee the future only when it coincides with their own wishes, and the most grossly obvious facts can be ignored when they are unwelcome.

George Orwell

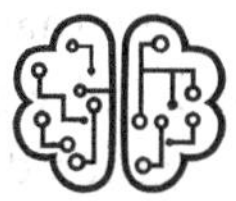

Consumption is at the heart of the economy and, it follows, marketing and advertising. But what happens when the way we consume changes fundamentally? We asked a panel of future-thinking researchers, practitioners and commentators some specific questions around this premise and here is what they had to say.

9.1 Technological Transformers

By Professor Wolfgang Henseler

Professor Henseler is Founder and Managing Creative Director of SENSORY-MINDS, a design studio for new media and innovative technologies based in Offenbach, Germany. He is also a Professor for Digital Media and an expert in digital transformation, user-centricity and user experience and the Dean for

K. Nelson-Field, *The Attention Economy and How Media Works*,
https://doi.org/10.1007/978-981-15-1540-8_9

Intermedia Design (the design of smart objects and the Internet of Things) at the University of Pforzheim/Germany, Faculty for Design.

His future view kicks off at a point where HAL 9000 meets The Truman Story. A place called Internet 4.0.

When we embrace Internet 4.0, we stand at an evolutionary pivot point for commerce. If we look at Amazon and their corporate vision to be the most customer-centric company in the world, we can see that we're closer than we think. Amazon's core attributes, like fast, simple, convenient, best usability, utmost user experience, already display the characteristics of a new type of marketplace. When Internet 4.0 starts to work well, it won't be just about the products anymore. It will be about the distinctiveness in service excellence that will make marketplaces relevant to users. Technology stops being the end game, it becomes the means with which we can best solve our problems.

As our retail and commerce system moves towards a foundation of user-centred thinking, it becomes interesting to look at the biggest manipulators of direction. History shows us that it will be a battle between enterprises and regulators. On the one hand we have the enterprises that run the IoT platforms where user data is gathered, analysed and converted into relevant products or services. On the other hand regulatory institutions will (sometimes belatedly) try to control the social, moral and ethical borders as enterprises keep nudging outwards, especially regarding artificial intelligence combined with algorithmic decision-making. When things start to think, AI regulations may be the only way to prevent future algorithms from manipulating us on their own. Welcome to HAL 9000.

So, can we rely on Hollywood and HAL 9000 to show us what the possible consequences might be for us humans? Yes and no. It's true that people will not be able to distinguish between real and artificial, this is happening now. Even in our current 3.0 digital world, the majority of users aren't aware of what kind of data they share and how this data is being used to manipulate them. Companies that are able to run user-centric systems in combination with artificially intelligent decision-making will lead the charge for a new wave of consumption. They will create a user-centred paradise where customers will have the best user experience they can imagine, even experiences they didn't imagine. But like all types of paradise it will be painful to leave, just like in the movie *The Truman Story*. It's hard to give up the things that make your life easy.

This new model of retail is based on consistently meeting people's needs before they are voiced; an outsourcing of wants and needs almost. In an Internet 4.0 marketplace that operates perfectly (or close to perfectly) we could see a much more sustainable usage of resources for creating products or services, and less inefficiency in production, marketing and logistics. Shops displaying rows of products aren't the most efficient means of distribution. But it's about more than consistently meeting people's needs, algorithmic influence will inspire people with products and services in a way that is satisfying for the customer. This requires a pretty complex understanding of the human customer. The Internet 4.0 enterprise will need to pre-empt and solve a human problem in an unexpected way.

And we're closer than you think. Companies like Amazon, Google or Alibaba are pretty much aware how beneficial user-centricity, user experience and using IoT technologies to solve human pain points, can be for their economic growth. The rest of the enterprises or governments are on their way to understanding digitisation; some have already built their big picture of what digitisation will mean to them and how to transfer this vision into reality. I would say that most of the companies are between 3–4 on a scale of 10.

Measurement becomes even more important in this new retail context. The traditional Customer Satisfaction Index will no longer be enough to measure the complexities of the new system. A new index will be required that predicts user behaviour based on user-centric principles using algorithm as its base—the Situative Relevance Index (SRI). Successful companies will combine IoT technologies with user-centric thinking. They will stop relying on self-reported happiness as a measure of success and start to incorporate deeper measures of service, function and relevance. These deeper SRI measures will also start to inform robo-advisors and smartbots.

We start to see that in a data-driven retail economy, it's no longer about (big) data. It's about the information in the data, and the machine learning competence we develop to use it for real-time algorithmic driven decision-making and situative relevant predictive services. Like so many commodities, the value is less in the raw commodity. The more we learn about how to process and use data as a commodity, the greater its value becomes.

The next 5–10 years will see an extraordinarily fundamental shift in how, what and where we buy and build things. The winners will be the ones who master extracting the value from data for user benefits the fastest.

9.2 The Problems

By Bob Hoffman

Bob is the author of four Amazon #1 selling books about advertising. He is also one of the most sought-after international speakers on advertising and marketing. He has brought us The Ad Contrarian blog since 2007. Bob has been the CEO of two independent agencies and the US operation of an international agency. In 2012 he was selected 'Ad Person of the Year' by the San Francisco Advertising Club. His commentary has appeared in the BBC World Service, The Wall Street Journal, MSNBC, The Financial Times, The Australian, New Zealand Public Broadcasting, Fox News, Sky News, Forbes, Canadian Public Broadcasting, and many other news outlets throughout the world.

His dystopian future is equal parts entertaining and frightening.

To whoever finds this,

It's been six years since I was arrested and held in this camp.

I often wonder what my wife and daughter think. One Tuesday evening I didn't come home. Do they think I deserted them? Do they think I'm dead? I guess by now they've gotten used to the idea that they'll never see me again.

I don't know how many people there are here but it seems like thousands. I've been told that there are dozens of these camps here in California and hundreds throughout the country. But we don't get news here so every rumour carries more weight than it probably should.

I never expected to be imprisoned. I had always been a rules-following, tax-paying, wage-earning citizen who didn't make trouble. How I got here is a story that would never have been believed before The Problems began.

Back in the early 2020s there were two trends in our country that seemed to be unrelated but as we now know somehow merged to create the situation we find ourselves in.

First there was deep political polarisation. The left kept getting lefter and the right kept getting righter. Although it was a period of unpleasantness, it really didn't seem unusually dangerous. There has always been a tenuous balance between right and left here in the US and this seemed to be just a mildly more intense strain of the natural disease of politics.

The second, seemingly unrelated, factor was the rise of what was called 'data-driven marketing'. The marketing industry believed that by having more information about us they could communicate with us in a more persuasive fashion. To get more information, they developed technology to follow us in our everyday activities. It was called 'tracking'.

They tracked what we read, who we corresponded with, what we said in our correspondence, where we went, and what we did. At the time we didn't think much of it because in return for tracking they provided us with some very useful and, frankly, fun and interesting stuff. We didn't really foresee how this could go wrong.

There were several companies back then that were particularly good at tracking and had collected a very large amount of information about people. The two most successful were called Google and Facebook. They had information about every person in the country. For the most part they kept their information private and it didn't seem to have much effect on our everyday lives.

I guess we might have foreseen that sooner or later there would be a rupture in society. History has an unambiguous lesson about governments: sooner or later every one of them is overthrown and replaced. I don't know why we thought we were exempt from this.

In any event, when The Problems arose and the major political parties collapsed, The Caretakers stepped into calm the turbulence. In order to root out the troublemakers, The Caretakers confiscated the records of Google and Facebook and all the other marketing companies.

There must have been something I wrote or something someone wrote about me that raised a red flag. Maybe it was my injudicious musings about all the data that was being collected falling into the wrong hands. And here I am.

I'm going to bury this now in the hope that someday it will be found. If you find this, please try to locate Janet and Nina Hoffman in San Francisco California and tell them I'm okay and I love them.

Bob Hoffman
Spring (I think) 2027

9.3 Hope After AdTech

By Augustine Fou

Dr. Fou is an independent cybersecurity and ad fraud researcher who helps clients identify and remove fraud impacting their marketing campaigns. He is an industry-recognised thought leader in digital strategy and integrated marketing. Dr. Fou was the former Chief Digital Officer of Omnicom's Healthcare Consultancy Group, a US$100 million agency group serving pharma, medical *device, and healthcare clients. He has also served as SVP, digital strategy lead, at McCann Worldgroup/MRM Worldwide. Dr. Fou taught digital strategy at NYU's School of Continuing and Professional Studies and Rutgers University's Center for Management Development. He started his career in New York City with McKinsey & Company.*

Augustine takes us through the fall and rise of AdTech.

Everything looks bleak right now.

Most people in digital AdTech may not agree with the statement that things look bleak right now. But then again, the people of Pompeii didn't see Vesuvius coming either. Not only is a crash coming for AdTech, but I think the crash is necessary. The digital marketing that we are doing now is not marketing at all. It is a gargantuan waste of money based on a layered-cake of ignorance, false assumptions, misunderstandings and conflicts of interest. The current vested interests are so deeply rooted that small incremental fixes will not turn digital marketing around; it will take a complete crash and do-over to fix digital marketing.

Why so pessimistic? I have studied digital marketing since the very beginnings of the public internet in the mid-1990s. I am a scientist by training, so I look for evidence, not opinion, to prove or disprove hypotheses. By looking back, we can start to see why digital marketing is in such a bad place now.

According to data from Pew Internet over the past 20 years, in the years since 2013, US internet and mobile usage appear to have plateaued. But the digital ad spend continues to move upward at an increasing rate. Digital ads are supposed to be shown to humans, when they visit websites and use their mobile devices. How did digital ad spend shoot up so much when human usage has already flat-lined?

Let's consider the basic law of supply and demand. Over the past 25 years, ad budgets have poured into digital from other advertising channels like TV, print and radio. Yet even with this unprecedented surge in demand we have seen overall decrease in average CPM prices. Despite the large influx of dollars into digital, CPM prices went down because supply grew even faster than the demand. With the rise of the ad exchanges, cyber criminals were also able to automate their fraud and drive unprecedented scale. Marketers, eager for larger volumes of ads to buy—to increase their reach and frequency—gobbled up this drastic increase in the number of available impressions. What they didn't realise at the time was their ads were being shown to bots, not humans.

This massive increase in supply absorbed all the dollars shifting into digital, and it was completely disconnected from human usage of media. Marketers became addicted to buying enormous amounts of ad impressions at artificially low prices. It's literally like crack cocaine, there was no going back. This addiction actually caused marketers to spend more money on fake ads which further increased their wasted ad spend and reduced their real outcomes. It wasn't until P&G cut US$200 million from their digital ad budgets that they saw it was entirely wasted. There was no change in business outcomes. The harm doesn't even stop there. The fake, inflated volumes, as well as fake bot-clicks are recorded in analytics. So digital campaigns are being optimised using completely erroneous analytics.

The catalyst for a crash is already visible—privacy regulation. GDPR (the EU's General Data Protection Regulation) and CCPA (California Consumer Privacy Act) are both starting to take effect. With these new laws, companies can be fined for the illicit collection and trade of private and personal information. The enforcement of these regulations may interpret, '...the list of sites that a user visits', to be personal information; and setting tracking cookies without consent to be in violation of the law. This means that practically all of AdTech would be illegal because its very foundation is built on collecting behavioural data, setting cookies, and being able to deliver targeted ads to individual people (identified by cookies) based on such information.

If enforcement of these regulations kicks into high gear and violations are successfully prosecuted, some AdTech companies will be fined heavily. This may trigger a cascading effect of companies going bankrupt, which in turn means larger aggregators upstream from them will also fail to make timely payments. And this starts the cycle which takes down the current 'AdTech industrial complex' as we know it now. The AdTech companies that were based on surveillance marketing will blow up and go away.

When we wake up after the AdTech crash, should we drop digital marketing like a hot potato?

I don't think so. Digital marketing itself isn't bad. In fact, it could be the best and most advanced form of marketing in human history. The true promise of digital has not yet been fulfilled. It promised unprecedented measurability and tracking that no other one-way media could deliver. Note that unprecedented measurability and infinite data are completely useless when the data is wrong or generated artificially by the actions of bots.

So, until we blow up ad fraud, we are not doing real digital marketing. The true promise of digital marketing has yet to be fulfilled. That day cannot come soon enough. What are you doing to hasten its arrival?

9.4 How *Will* Brands Grow?

By Professor Karen Nelson-Field

There is no denying the scale of transformation heading our way. The experts, including our futurists, are predicting it will be extreme and wide reaching. Professor Henseler has heralded the rising importance of functionality, Dr Fou has warned of the imminent AdTech crash and Mr Hoffman gave us a clue as to why the crash needs to happen. I'm an optimist, so while I agree that all of these things will happen, I also advocate that new growth will emerge from the AdTech crash and burn. This growth will be shaped by the giant e-commerce aggregators like JD.com, Alibaba and Amazon. A very large part of our future buying will be restricted to a few players and a very large part of our advertising dollars will be assigned to them. Bricks and mortar sites will significantly diminish and the greatest physical presence of these new retailers will be the delivery drone. Our ever-increasing desire for convenience is about to step up a notch and change everything.

Amazon, Alibaba and JD.com are pioneers of, and will indisputably become best in the world at, continuous learning and real-time personalisation. Success will be predicted within an inch of its life where success means an actual sale, not brand favourability, brand recall or intention to buy. This will change everything we know about how marketers distribute and market their brands and how customers will make brand choices.

So, where does this leave brands? Will consumers really shift their trust from product brands to distributor brands? Will we be asking Alexa or Siri to order instant coffee or will we ask for Nescafe? When we start to divest ourselves of the number of consumer decisions we make in a day what, if anything, will change?

The changes we are about to see will be a fundamental disruption to the way in which we buy and sell things. A scarier thought is that they could disrupt the way we *want* things. The decline or success of a brand will now be attached in some way to the algorithmic editor. Regardless of how that actually plays out, within 10 years we will be forced to reconsider the laws of brand growth, within 20 years they will be vastly different. Consumers will still buy products, that will never change, but the parameters around penetration and loyalty as they stand today, will. And these parameters will change because the algorithms are designed to build filter bubbles around us to ensure that success is achieved. This means curation of information by the algorithmic editor will expose us to fewer product options (and given the overload of choice and information, that will probably be a relief). As such our buying repertoires will become significantly smaller and brand switching will no longer be typical.

We will be more loyal to one because we will have been relinquished of a large portion of our consumer decision-making brain power. But don't confuse this with brand loyalty, rather, we will be loyal to the functionality of the product. Brand growth will no longer come from getting many light buyers to buy you once more, and supercharged recency planning and distribution mechanisms will replace the need for driving Mental Availability. These e-commerce platforms (and the vast associated advertising and content platforms they own) will become our main source of advertising exposure, and our attention to advertising will be even lower. Marketing budgets will be largely assigned to physical availability to fuel the ratings algorithms and many media platforms will die.

How exactly a brand grows in this environment is anyone's guess. The traditional advantages of being a big brand are disappearing with small brands already appearing on the same stage. Perhaps, there will be a longer tail of small products that are sustained within their own loyal ecosystem. And perhaps brands will no longer be needed, we will buy simply for function over desire. Although the human need to compare with others is pretty strong, so it's hard to believe that desire will disappear.

The laws of brand growth were discovered at a time when advertising exposure was scattergun and product distribution options were vast. It feels like the net is tightening and the future marketplace will turn this on its head.

We need to be open minded, just as Vitruvius was in the first century.

Index

K. Nelson-Field, *The Attention Economy and How Media Works*, https://doi.org/10.1007/978-981-15-1540-8